The Children's Media Yearbook is a publication of The Children's Media Foundation
Director, Greg Childs
Administrator, Jacqui Wells

The Children's Media Foundation
P.O. Box 56614
London W13 0XS
info@thechildrensmediafoundation.org

First published 2014

ISBN 978-0-9575518-2-4 Paperback

ISBN 978-0-9575518-3-1 E-book

Book design by Craig Taylor
Cover illustration by Stuart Harrison
Previous page illustration by CBeebies/Beakus

The Children's Media Yearbook 2014

Edited by Lynn Whitaker

THE CHILDREN'S MEDIA FOUNDATION

INTRODUCTION

INDUSTRY NEWS AND VIEWS

Editorial
Lynn Whitaker 01

Welcome to the 2014 issue of *The Children's Media Yearbook*, with which I hope to build on the success of last year's inaugural issue. Published by the Children's Media Foundation (CMF), a not-for-profit body dedicated to ensuring quality in children's media provision, each yearbook provides an overview of the live issues in children's media over a twelve-month period, with a particular emphasis on the UK context. It serves, therefore, as a snapshot of contemporary children's media discourses as they emerge and evolve year on year – whether in relation to policy, production, consumption or education – and seeks to represent news, views and comment from the diverse range of stakeholders in children's media across all platforms. It is a one of a kind publication in that respect, and an ambitious undertaking by the CMF, but the reception and uptake of the book would confirm that it is a worthwhile endeavour offering something to parents, researchers, producers and policy makers alike.

There is more on the work of the CMF in this introductory section as Chair, Anna Home, presents her round-up of the year's activities and Founder Patron, Brian Jameson, explains his decision to become involved. It should be stressed however that my role as editor is a fully independent one (I am a media academic researching at the nexus of policy and production concerns) and that the yearbook *as a whole* does not necessarily represent the views of the CMF as an organisation. Rather, the yearbook deliberately sets out to present diverse standpoints and so fulfils the educational or civic remit of the CMF to facilitate and encourage informed discussion and quality debate on what can often be contentious issues around children's media. Contributors are chosen and invited with a view to creating balance and contrast within each section, as well as across the book as a whole, even though readers may, of course, choose to simply dip in and out of articles or sections that are of greatest interest.

As such, I have invited my contributors to 'tell their own stories'; some do so by blowing their own horn and others by beating a drum (they can be a noisy lot). Where competing voices and agendas are most at odds it is for readers to make up their own minds and it could be said that, while the children's media ecology has fast-changing platforms and technologies, often its tensions are the perennial ones around commercialism, quality, representation, and the competing imperatives of education and entertainment: tensions that have existed for as long as we have had media (dedicated or otherwise) for children.

Still, the mood and tone would seem a positive one, on the whole, with producers, policy makers, academics and parents finding much that is praiseworthy in the current UK children's media landscape, even when this is tempered by critique. In particular, high quality, dedicated children's content is celebrated throughout the articles in this book and innovation, creativity and diversity is championed.

The first main section of the book, then, presents inside news and views from industry: contributions from content producers (large and small) who operate within the UK, and representatives from the trade bodies that form part of that content supply, distribution and funding picture. Joe Godwin is joined this year by Kay Benbow and Cheryl Taylor to tell us all that's fresh at BBC Children's, while Louise Bucknole paints the picture for Disney's portfolio of channels in the UK. While coming from separate public service and commercial standpoints (and celebrating different goals and successes accordingly) both these articles convey something of the vibrancy of dedicated children's channels and both place emphasis on knowing their audience.

These articles are followed by the somewhat more personal viewpoints of Steve Smith and Danny Stack. Steve writes of his passion and commitment in running Beakus, an animation studio based in London. It's an entertaining and wholly candid insight into the challenges and rewards of navigating the tricky waters of the animation industry and I'm particularly grateful to Steve for illustrating the critical importance of the UK animation tax breaks. Danny Stack also talks from his personal experience of writing for children's television, in an exuberant piece that nonetheless demonstrates the hard graft, talent and grit required of being a professional writer specialising in children's content.

The section is rounded off by a trio of pieces presenting different aspects of the commercial realities of the children's media industry. I was very pleased that Kelvyn Gardner agreed to contribute his honest account of the sometimes maligned licensing sector and hope that inclusion within the yearbook can promote better understanding of licensing's role. Likewise Natasha Crookes's article, on behalf of the British Toy and Hobby Association, sets out the work of this trade body and its often direct connections to children's media products. The BTHA were invited to participate this year as I am keen to show the broader context in which children's media is produced and consumed. The final article in the section introduces another new strand to the yearbook – children's publishing – from Julia Posen of Walker Books. I set Julia something of a challenge with her brief: rather than give a general overview of Walker's activities, I asked her to specifically address the topic of gender. She does so engagingly and having such an honest piece from a content provider of the stature of Walker Books makes for thought-provoking reading.

The second substantive section, 'Policy and Research' can be seen as where the CMF's remit and my own are perhaps most closely aligned: we aim to put policy and research at the centre of discourse and debate. As an academic in this sphere I know it can be frustrating that there is no single place to which one can point as a statement of policy (research-driven or otherwise) affecting children's media. I hope that, year on year, the contributions of different policy makers and regulators can help build a picture of the diverse forces that shape children's media in the UK.

This year we are joined by three regulatory authorities and the section starts with David Austin setting out the (very interesting) work of the British Board of Film Classification. The next piece, by Marie Southgate, brings us up to date on the Office of Fair Trading investigation into what is often referred to as children's 'in-app purchasing'. This was a big news story for the games industry in the last year and Marie explains the findings and how the new Competition & Markets Authority (CMA) will take forward compliance issues. Next, Alison Preston, having last year given a fulsome account of the entire spectrum of Ofcom's activities relevant to children's media, now focuses specifically on their research into children's media use and attitudes. I think what this, and the preceding two 'institutional' pieces underline, is the importance of empirical research in policy making. 'Policy' and 'research' are not two separate categories.

The section continues with three individual pieces from leading academic researchers in children's media. Sonia Livingstone draws on her most recent research projects on children's online media use to ask what we mean by 'good' content for children. Barbie Clarke also addresses the online children's sphere, with research conducted to coincide with 'Safer Internet Day' in February this year. But lest we worry that all the attention is directed towards the internet, I asked Cynthia Carter to contribute her specific area of expertise with an article on children's television news provision, which makes a powerful point regarding the continuing centrality of the medium of television. The final piece in the section comes from Colin Ward on behalf of the CMF. Colin underlines the CMF's aim to promote balanced research-led debate via its online 'Parent Portal', but gives a somewhat tongue in cheek reminder of the legitimate limits and uses of research. It stands then not as a counterpoint to, but an endorsement of, all the preceding articles wherein all contributors, whether academic or institutional, place emphasis on 'the voice of the child' and use 'real life' research with children as a central methodology.

The last of our three main sections, 'Commentary and Debate' is where contributors are invited to really make their critique explicit. The section opens with Mark Sorrell's piece on making money out of children. He pulls no punches in this hilarious but nonetheless incisive examination of everything from games to gambling for children. The torch passes then to Gary Pope, who, speaking from his perspective as a parent, comments further on ideas of value, quality and ethics in 'monetising childhood'. Gary's piece can be read as an open letter to the content industries to take care in their brand development strategies, illustrated with some bad practice.

Stuart Dredge focuses next on all that is good, new and exciting in apps for children, with several caveats to that assessment particularly from his parental experience. Another parental view is given by Helen Simmons, who offers what she sees as the typical experiences of a parent trying to do right by their child and their media choices and she raises many of the questions that CMF have found to be most often asked by parents. This is followed then by two distinct clarion calls for industry change: Alex Lewis Paul's account of the Let Toys Be Toys campaign and Beth Cox's indictment of what she sees as the growing gender issues in children's publishing. Robert Keeley also speaks of the children's publishing industry, rounding off the section with his upbeat account of how self-publishing can make a positive impact and has become a force to be reckoned with.

As with last year's issue, the yearbook closes with a 'Farewell' section containing obituaries of those leading lights in children's media who have died in the preceding twelve-month period. In addition to the obituaries we remember leading institutions or texts and I invited Richard Marson to write a retrospective of BBC Television Centre and Paul R. Jackson to reflect on the 50th anniversary of *Play School*. It is fitting then that a reflective 'Afterword' was offered by Justin Fletcher, one of our most-loved contemporary preschool presenters, to bring both this article, and the yearbook to a close. (And at the back you can find biographies of all our contributors – including Justin, and our fabulous cover artist, Stuart Harrison – who each give their content for free.)

Plans are, of course, already underway for the 2015 issue and I am always delighted to receive suggestions or contributions of material for any of the sections. I especially welcome feedback, and ideas for new strands or areas, so please get in touch (my details are at the back too) and see you next year!

The Children's Media Foundation Year Two

Anna Home

02

In our second year, we have consolidated our structure and clarified our remit, focusing on specific areas of work.

The Executive Committee groups have developed their roles and activities: for example, the Research Group has commissioned and developed the Parent Portal, launched on our website, www.thechildrensmediafoundation.org, in March. The portal provides a number of responses to the questions we discovered parents most want to ask about the media their kids consume, and the responses reflect a variety of academic views on the subject. This service to parents and other interested parties is part of our policy to inform the public about different academic opinions being advanced on issues in children's media, giving people the opportunity to make their own informed decisions.

The current CMF Executive Committee is as follows:
APPG – Jayne Kirkham
Communications – Anthony Utley
Diversity – Angela Ferreira
Industry Liaison – Martin Franks
Online / Interactive – Marc Goodchild
Policy – Mark Pallis
Research – Colin Ward
Supporter Development and Events – Matt Deegan

The events group launched its inaugural programme with a lively debate on the BBC Trust's report on children's services. This was followed by another on the issues of diversity and gender representation in children's media – you'll find articles on this topic in the 'Commentary and Debate' section of this book – and in March we co-hosted with BAFTA a successful event on the future of children's film, 'We Need to Talk About Children's Film', with speakers from the British Council film team, the BFI, Mind Candy and Vertigo Films.

Film has indeed been one of our main concerns this year; we welcomed the appointment by the BFI of Justin Johnson, who is to research and write an in-depth report on the status quo of the children's and young people's part of the industry. This report is due to be published in the autumn and we hope it will lead to some positive new thinking – and new initiatives! The APPG for Children's Media and the Arts (chaired by Floella Benjamin and for which the CMF political liaison group provides the Secretariat) will hold a session on this report when it has been published. One of the APPG's highlights during the year was a discussion on Beeban Kidron's film *In Real Life*, which examines the use of the internet by young people and raises issues regarding appropriate content and safety – another of our ongoing concerns and addressed later in this yearbook in contributions from Sonia Livingstone and Barbie Clarke.

During the year we have continued to build alliances and relationships with other organisations with concerns in our field such as Ofcom; Pact; VLV; COBA, the BBFC and PhonepayPlus. We believe very strongly in cooperation wherever possible.

Communication is crucial and CMF have improved and extended our website, and our communication via Twitter and Facebook, in order to keep in touch with both the general public and our supporters. This idea of 'keeping in touch' works both ways.

Looking ahead it is clear that the major issue, for next year and beyond, will be the long-term future, financing and structure of the BBC. There is already considerable debate going on in the press and elsewhere and positions are being taken up. The BBC itself is making radical proposals such as the move of BBC Three online, which has long-term implications, especially for children growing up and moving (or not) into its target audience.

The BBC is a national institution of great importance and the debate needs to be measured and serious. We intend to play our part in that debate and will be consulting with industry, parents and young people on this issue.

It is CMF's role to ensure that, whatever happens, the interests of the children's audience are protected and the quality and quantity of content not eroded.

Given all that is going on, the relevance of CMF is clear. We are still a small, mainly volunteer, organisation and we need to continue to raise our profile and maintain continuity in our activities. Special mention should be given to our bash to celebrate 50 years of *Play School*, held at Riverside Studios in May. One of the key themes of that event was the idea of continuity and legacy in UK children's media and we expand on that theme throughout this book.

I want to thank everyone who has worked so hard over the year to help us get to this point, and also to all those who support us financially, especially our Founder Patrons new and old – we need you and we are really grateful!

Finally I want to pay tribute to Jocelyn Hay whose obituary is included in this issue. She was a great campaigner for quality media in general and always supported the cause of excellent media for children. She leaves a great example of how to make a difference.

A Founder Patron's View 03
Brian Jameson

As a newly paid up Founder Patron of the Children's Media Foundation, I have finally put my money where my mouth is. It's payback time for the huge fun and kicks I get out of producing programmes for preschool children.

But my path wasn't always such. RADA trained, National Theatre Player, I was an actor first and foremost. For twenty years I plied my trade.

Like any jobbing actor, in order to make a decent living between treading the boards and motivating in front of the camera, one had to have a sideline. Mine was recording language lessons for the BBC World Service; asking, "Where's the way to the lavatory?" in my best Standard English, honed my craft. The extra dosh was useful and the lunches at Bush House were legendary.

Then, on an actor's afternoon, sitting watching *Play School* with my children, I thought, "I could do that. That might be another useful little sideline."

So, one day, whilst performing some '70s sex comedy in Harrogate, I put my clothes back on and dashed down to TV Centre for a *Play School* audition. There I met the wonderful Cynthia Felgate and a young studio director called Greg Childs.

When I announced my piece for my camera audition Greg warned me, "She won't like that! We've had ten of those already this morning." Heeding the first of Greg's lifetime of warnings, I asked Cynthia if I could do my own story. Cynthia bit into her cream cracker, broke the rules and said, "Oh, go on then!"

So I told a story about a woolly hairy spider who thought the screams he elicited from people were a sign of love. The woolly spider brought me luck – I passed the audition and joined the merry band of *Play School* players.

With my new role, I eased off visits to Bush House and the sideline began to consume.

What I loved about *Play School* was the total collective dedication to the audience. As an actor I could relate to that. Also, the presenters, musicians, directors and producers – a diverse and highly talented bunch – were enormous fun to be with. The very young audience was no different from the older clientele at the National Theatre – loved a bit of verse, appreciated characterisation and hooted if you fell on your bottom.

So consumed was I with this new sideline that I even turned down a West End play in order to host a batch of episodes. Such was the power of *Play School*.

Pivotal in all this was Cynthia Felgate. Also an actor, she chose her teams well. Never the voice of negative, she allowed and encouraged the impossible to happen. And for me, once again, the impossible did happen – something I never looked for or dreamed of. One month I was playing 'Buttons' with the stars of *On the Buses* (ever the jobbing actor) then next I was in a BBC multi-camera studio as a director. How did that suddenly happen? It was magic!

As a director on *Play School*, you wrote your own script and you owned your slot. There was no better nor more privileged life than coming up with ideas and guiding your visions through to their conclusion on screen. There was no better audience than the preschool child free from the confines of learnt appreciation.

There was no better group of people than the *Play School* producers to help you improve your craft. The possibilities were endless with no one telling you, "You can't do this" or "You can't do that." Just wonderful arguments with Greg Childs or Christine Hewitt who would always end up saying, "Well, do it then!" *Play School* for me was a negativity-free zone from start to finish.

When the show ended and Cynthia began *Playdays* as an independent, I joined her company at its inception. I was a writer, director, producer and an actor playing the *Playdays* bus driver. Ridiculous! I soon dropped the actor bit. I was now totally consumed by and passionate about preschool programme production and so my sideline became my life.

Under Cynthia's guidance the *Play School* principles still continued. Freed up from the confines of BBC practice, and being one of the first independent producers, we could take advantage of all that was new at the time. Central to this was our young audience and its diversity. They needed more of a voice and to be included in the programmes themselves. We tried out many new ideas; they didn't always work but we continued to pioneer. We produced the first preschool musical; we featured the first preschool presenter with a disability; and we produced the first preschool programme made entirely in an Irish travellers' camp, way before *My Big Fat Gypsy Wedding*. When Cynthia died it was a huge loss for preschool programming. But for those of us who had come into contact with her and who were from the *Play School* stable, there was still a reference.

Creating *Balamory* was totally in the *Play School* tradition. Multi-layered and inclusive, it was designed to engage a range of abilities and ages. The very young could enjoy it with no need to grasp the narrative; older children could join the programme at any time and quickly catch up with the story. Adults sharing their child's viewing – alas, too few – could appreciate the shenanigans of the soap opera-like characters. An Irish traveller watching would also feel included with the heartbeat bodhran thumping away in the opening titles.

Cynthia had founded one of the first of the new 'indies'. Many of her protégée presenters and directors followed in her wake and created their own successful companies. Again I thought, "I can do that!" and – very *Play School* – made a moon from a potato. Together with Helen Doherty we founded the first Scottish preschool indie, 'Tattiemoon'. For me, running a company is still about having a vision and guiding it through to its conclusion as one did with each individual *Play School* episode.

Play School was my foundation in children's programming, but today talent can abound with no direct reference to it. Why should it? Technology offers exciting, weird, wonderful and ever newer ways of enhancing narrative. There are myriad platforms too for communicating our visions and giving the audience the choice of when and where and how to view.

A long time ago Cynthia broke the rules and gave me the chance to tell my own story, all about a woolly spider. There was just me talking to camera and telling the tale. Thirty years later I told the tale again but in a different way. A very realistic 3D animated spider scampers around and interacts with a three year old child. Woolly is now the star of his own CBeebies show, *Woolly and Tig*.

Woolly and Tig is on CBeebies daily but his popularity became immediately apparent on another platform – the iPlayer. For choice the iPlayer is a young child's dream, where they can access and watch their favourite programme over and over again. Woolly can also be discovered scampering on his own app, on his own web show, and soon to be heard on his own radio show. That audition piece, that story, has come a long way and adapted to the challenges and opportunities of the modern media landscape. Cynthia's legacy remains though and so the story rules.

Possibilities are endless even within financial restraints. But reference is needed not only from the past but ahead of the game too. The audience is as vulnerable as ever and care is always called for.

Working practices too have changed. In indies we are far flung, working in isolation in our shoebox accommodation. 'Touching base' happens in the ether with us rarely actually seeing each other. Arguments and debate are few and short. We want to please the corporate, the licensee, the commissioners and the co-producer. We rush from conferences to meetings to ten-minute windows. We lack fresh air and space.

In our efforts to become pluralistic, we can become bland. In our efforts to prove our expertise, we can revel in the list of all the things you can't do and ignore the infinite unexplored possibilities of things you can do. We can focus on the child with the iPad and forget the child with the pit bull.

In this complex – even exploitative – media world, CMF is an organisation that champions and protects children's interests, makes sense of the complexities, and provides a point of reference for the creative. We need such organisations more than ever.

Looking to the future and to new possibilities, a sure-fire edict is that children love to watch other children. Not children as props giving a collective wave but individual children of their own age and from their own culture intrinsically involved with the programme. For preschool that is a huge challenge and it was on the agenda way back doing *Playdays*. We have a come a long way since then, and much has been achieved, but the restrictions of shooting schedules, licensing laws and budget restraints means we have hardly begun to explore the possibilities. I would love to further develop this exciting area and draw on my experience to create a new drama centred entirely around and using three and four year olds. It would cost!

But hey, you never know. Magic does happen. Meanwhile I put my money where my mouth is and support CMF where the child is centre stage, always.

tattiemoon

BBC Children's
Joe Godwin, Kay Benbow and Cheryl Taylor

Joe Godwin, Director, BBC Children's

2013-14 was quite a year for BBC Children's. As we approach our third birthday based in the North in May, we've launched our first mobile app for CBeebies, and earlier this year CBeebies Land at Alton Towers opened its doors to our legions of fans and their families. The future is here, but we never forget our past – this year is also the fiftieth anniversary of the iconic *Play School* – and a major exhibition on the history of BBC Children's will open at The Lowry theatre and gallery in Manchester this summer.

As the debate about the future of the BBC and charter renewal begins, high quality British children's content remains one of the BBC's key editorial priorities. In their positive and supportive review of the Children's services in 2013, the BBC Trust endorsed our strategy of ensuring our content is accessible to as many children as possible, to do even more to broaden the appeal of our content, and to work with colleagues across the BBC to better promote our TV web and radio content.

We invest over £100 million a year in our TV and online services for children. Producing ad-free, original UK content is what sets us apart from other broadcasters, and kids and their families tell us that's what they value and love.

Our aim is to be inclusive in everything and we want every child in the UK to see a life a bit like their own reflected. It's a responsibility we take seriously in Children's and we think it shows. We introduce challenging issues that help children to learn and we don't underestimate our audience, whether it's physics for four year olds or having Dick and Dom explain Archimedes.

Even though the UK has one of the most complicated and competitive children's media markets in the world, CBeebies and CBBC are the undisputed favourite channels for their target audiences. I find this reassuring; children actively seek out challenging and inspiring content. They don't always choose the easiest watch, and love to see and hear other British children.

Watching TV is still most children's favourite recreational activity, but also they're spending more and more time online and adopting new viewing habits that change the way we think about delivering our content. Nearly three quarters of homes with children have a tablet device, and children are leading the way with on demand viewing. I'm not worried about these changing habits; we just need to understand them and make sure our content is where children want to consume it. It's vitally important that the BBC understands this, as these are the mainstream habits of tomorrow.

This makes it even more important that we make sure our online services are safe for children; but we have a responsibility to help kids learn how to be safe wherever they are on the web. CBBC's *Dixi*, as well as being an innovative, exciting online drama, is a brilliant way to encourage children to think about their data and their safety when using social media.

2014 has already brought a number of awards we are all incredibly proud of because our work is being recognised as the best in the world. After dragging a huge haul of BAFTAs back to Salford last November, in 2014 our TV programmes have already won awards at Broadcast Awards, Kidscreen, and the international Emmys.

2014 will continue to be a very big year for us – we have our second CBBC Live event, as, following on from last year's success in Leeds, we're doing it again in Newcastle. CBeebies Land is now open in Alton Towers, bringing our favourite CBeebies characters even closer to audiences who are able to visit.

Ninety-two years after the first BBC *Children's Hour*, on the new-fangled electric wireless, we're still here and still getting to grips with the future.

Kay Benbow, CBeebies Controller

CBeebies has been called a 'jewel in the crown of the BBC'. We broadcast innovative, high quality content to the BBC's youngest audience – content that engages and delights children and their families across TV, radio, online and mobile. Our priority at CBeebies is to ensure that our youngest viewers are offered a rich mix of diverse, ground-breaking and distinctive shows across our portfolio.

We are incredibly proud of our commitment to original British drama for preschoolers – something of a new genre for CBeebies. Drawing on the legacies of iconic books *Topsy & Tim*, we've created an authentic ongoing narrative, full of warmth and humour, inspired by the everyday experiences of children and families. The much-loved *Katie Morag* books have brought stories that celebrate community and family life, all shot on location in the beautiful Highlands and Islands of Scotland.

We continue to feature iconic actors in our shows: introducing a new generation to Bernard Cribbins in the magical *Old Jack's Boat* and James Bolam in the comedy drama *Grandpa in My Pocket*. The CBeebies

Bedtime Hour also attracts wonderfully talented performers ranging from Maxine Peake and Floella Benjamin to Damian Lewis and David Hasselhoff!

At CBeebies we are proud of producing shows that only the BBC would do. In *Magic Hands*, we've made TV history by bringing poetry to life for deaf and hearing children with music, animation and British Sign Language, performed by a cast of deaf presenters. *Melody* (played by ten year old Angharad Rhodes) uses classical music to inspire the imagination of children with particular relevance to those with visual impairments. In *Something Special*, our iconic and inclusive series, Justin Fletcher and Mr Tumble explore the world with children who have learning and communication difficulties.

This year we have increased the number of events and specials on CBeebies. Our annual Christmas Show is now an unmissable highlight and this season's offering was a beautiful production of *A Christmas Carol*, specially adapted for our young viewers and filmed in front of a live audience at the Crucible Theatre, Sheffield. A moving Christmas episode of *Old Jack's Boat* was much appreciated by our audience and their families, and both these productions performed well in the BBC1 Christmas schedule after premiering on CBeebies. Following last year's collaboration with Northern Ballet, in which we introduced our audience to dance with the time honoured classic *The Ugly Duckling*, we will soon be showing our ballet version of *The Three Little Pigs*. Complementary content supports all these specials in our continuity links, online, and on CBeebies Radio, extending and deepening the experience for our audience.

Learning through play is at the heart of CBeebies and we have a range of programmes that equip preschoolers with the skills they need. *Nina and the Neurons* presents challenging topics like geology and engineering in an engaging and accessible format. *Stargazing* introduced our audience to astronomy as part of the pan-BBC event. *Get Squiggling Letters* shows children how to form their letters, *Alphablocks* how to form words and *What's the Big Idea?* asks age-appropriate philosophical questions such as: "What is a Friend?"

And it's not just little ones we have in mind when we are producing content. *Time for School* offers support for parents, as well as children, for the transition to school. Then, in our interactive space, we really hear what families have to say. We have a thriving social media community of parents and carers with whom we have a regular dialogue – they share their praise and criticism of our output and we are able to communicate with and explain how our content can support them.

CBeebies strives to offer a connected journey between our now numerous platforms, whether it's complementary immersive online and mobile content for standout shows like *Andy's Dinosaur Adventures* and *Swashbuckle*, or activities and games on the 'CBeebies Playtime' App, which has now passed the 2 million download mark – a huge thrill for the CBeebies team.

We know that our audience love brilliant animation and we strive to give them the best. Award-winning titles *Rastamouse* and *Sarah and Duck* are just two of our distinctive animations that use appealing characters to solve problems to "make a bad ting good!" and ask questions that help children make sense of the world around them. These titles join other favourites like *Octonauts*, *Charlie and Lola*, *Mike the Knight*, *The Adventures of Abney and Teal*, *64 Zoo Lane*, *Timmy Time* and *Postman Pat*.

To maximise our resources and offer the best value for money we continue to seek collaborations with like-minded partners internally and externally. Some of our most successful, ground-breaking content is made in partnership, e.g. with BBC Learning (*Stargazing*, *Magic Hands*, *Melody*); BBC Worldwide/ BBC Natural History Unit (*Andy's Wild Adventures* and *Andy's Dinosaur Adventures*); Fremantle (*Tree Fu Tom*); and our most recent collaboration with Sesame Workshop, which sees Elmo and the Cookie Monster arrive on CBeebies, at *The Furchester Hotel*.

And to cap it all, CBeebies was voted Channel of the Year at the 2013 Children's BAFTA awards!

Cheryl Taylor, CBBC Controller

CBBC is the colourful and exclusive home of BBC content for six to twelve year olds. The channel is extremely popular and has the highest overall reach of any UK Children's channel with 30% of the target audience consuming content each week – that's around 1.5 million children.

CBBC provides a broad range of distinctive and stimulating TV and online content: from thrilling drama and comedy, through entertainment, absorbing factual and factual entertainment series, as well as a dedicated news service in *Newsround*.

Children from across the UK can enjoy different touch points with the channel and we are always working on new ways to increase accessibility.

Participation and portrayal are particularly important to us and as a public service broadcaster we feel it's vital that our audience can relate to our content and get involved with us in as many ways as possible.

Absorbing factual content remains central to the slate, with shows like *Operation Ouch* and *Dick and Dom's Absolute Genius* enlivening potentially dry subjects with vibrant production techniques and inspiring on-screen personalities.

We encourage our audience to embrace other countries and cultures with thought-provoking shows like *Extreme School*, *Show Me What You're Made Of*, and *All Over the Place*. The award winning *My Life* documentary strand follows the eye-opening stories of extraordinary young people who demonstrate inspirational courage or flair. This year's *Newsround* Specials have included reports from Afghanistan and a special feature on cyber bullying.

Shows like *Marrying Mum and Dad* continue to allow children to take the lead, and we were delighted to win a Stonewall Award in 2013 for featuring the same sex marriage of two dads – all organised by their three adopted children.

Drama remains a significant genre for our audience and recent highlights include *Wolfblood* and *Wizards vs Aliens*. *The Dumping Ground* continues to prove just as popular as channel stalwart *Tracy Beaker* and other successes include *Rocket's Island*, *Roy*, *4 O'Clock Club*, and the intriguing *The Sparticle Mystery*.

Drama has become a key area of co-production for us and the greater investment this engenders has meant increasingly high production values and levels of sophistication for our fiction-hungry audience.

Multi-award-winning *Horrible Histories* and *Friday Download* lead an enviable list of comedy and entertainment shows including all new *Hank Zipzer* (featuring a protagonist with dyslexia), *All at Sea*, *The Dog Ate my Homework*, *Dani's Castle*, *Johnny and Inel*, *Officially Amazing*, *The Daredevil* and *Sam & Mark's Big Friday Wind-Up*.

DNN (Definitely Not Newsround), *Help! My Supply Teacher is Magic* and *Hacker Time* also contributed to the diverse CBBC line-up along with the brand new UK-made animation, *Strange Hill High*.

And of course there is our most enduring friend: *Blue Peter*, the longest running Children's show of all time, which continues to premiere weekly on CBBC. The show inspires children to get involved with a wide range of culturally significant activities as well as physically challenging initiatives such as Radzi's Sport Relief Swim across Lake Windermere. Thousands joined in to vote Lindsey in as our new presenter in *Blue Peter – You Decide!*

Interactive content has become increasingly important for our audience, who expect to find their favourite brands when and where they want. More than half of homes with children in the UK now have a tablet device, and last year CBBC content generated over 200 million requests on iPlayer. The CBBC mobile site continues to expand its menu of scintillating video clips and games for phones and tablets. Our iPlayer offering becomes ever more sophisticated in response to burgeoning demand; *The Dumping Ground* series alone has attracted over 8 million requests in eight weeks.

The CBBC website facilitates deeper engagement with favourite brands and also allows users to connect with each other in a safe and creative environment. Our audience are currently engaged in new interactive experiences such as *Dixi* – the digital detective story which helps promote safer internet use – and new 'webisodes' for popular brands such as *The Dumping Ground* and *4 O'Clock Club*.

We'll be launching a suite of CBBC brand-related apps later this year to add to the successful launch of playalong app 'Ludus' early in 2013. This app uses state of the art audio-watermarking technology to enhance playalong capabilities on mobile devices and has proved a real success with our curious and adventurous audience.

top to bottom The Dumping Ground, Blue Peter Live in Leeds

The unique and effervescent on-screen presence of our continuity team in the CBBC office, along with our brilliant *Newsround* and *Blue Peter* presenters, offer young viewers wonderful and entertaining role models and many more opportunities to participate. They express their appreciation by sending thousands of letters and emails to us each year (10,000 in January 2014 alone!).

Following the success of 2013's CBBC *Live in Leeds*, we'll be giving viewers another opportunity to get involved with a similar event in Newcastle/Gateshead this spring. 40,000 people attended last time, and on this occasion families will get a chance to see their favourite presenters such as Sam and Mark, Hacker and the *Friday Download* team live, as well as take part in many other CBBC related activities.

We're incredibly proud of the huge range of captivating content we offer across an increasing number of platforms. Our audience can have fun, absorb challenging and sensitive subjects and – best of all – participate in all that CBBC has to offer in a safe, supportive and stimulating environment.

Katie Morag

Disney Channels UK 05
Louise Bucknole

For 90 years, Disney has enchanted audiences with its storytelling and magical characters that touch kids and families, young and old. Disney Channels have become one of the company's most powerful brand ambassadors and drivers of the first interaction today's kids have with the Disney brand through its portfolio of channels - Disney Junior, Disney Channel and Disney XD - which cater for two to eleven year olds.

One of the first things that struck me, when I joined Disney, was how the channels' rich portfolio of content with beautiful stories and iconic characters drive everything we do. Our mission is to build emotional connections – between content, the Disney audience, and the world in which they live. Disney's unwavering conviction is that the strongest emotional connections come from creating immersive content and amazing experiences.

Achieving this isn't easy and we have to be agile and dynamic in how we develop content by listening to how our audience is changing and responding to their needs. We must innovate using new ideas, approaches and technology to ensure our audience can enjoy, experience and interact with our properties in ways that are meaningful. Our audience, although young, is always evolving; and understanding how and adjusting what we do accordingly is a never-ending journey. We are fortunate to have a rich content heritage, which we are constantly evolving, expanding and re-imagining.

Disney Junior has an amazing range of quality content for preschoolers: from established favourites such as *Mickey Mouse Clubhouse* with its roots in mathematical puzzles, to our hit show about a princess in training, *Sofia the First*. We invite our youngest viewers into the world of Captain Hook and Peter Pan in *Jake and the Never Land Pirates*, and we enable them to share the experiences of a trainee doctor who nurtures her toys in *Doc McStuffins* – a show with a powerful role model, which was a major hit on a recent retail tour across the UK. An emerging theme for us is the re-imagining of iconic Disney characters to engage a new generation. Disney Junior already has some great examples of this, and a soon-to-launch new addition is *The 7D*, a new comedy about the seven dwarves out next year.

from left to right Sofia the First, Doc McStuffins, The 7D

For boys, we have a rich array of content and Disney XD's incredible adventures range from the number one ratings driver *Phineas & Ferb* to *Gravity Falls*, *Hulk and the Agents of S.M.A.S.H.*, *Ultimate Spider Man*, *Marvel's Avengers Assemble*, *Crash & Bernstein* and *Mighty Med*. Our Marvel Universe block is growing from strength to strength as new superheroes join the channel's line-up. This will be further strengthened this autumn with the premiere of Lucasfilm's hotly-anticipated CGI *Star Wars Rebels*, a show we are all very excited about!

For girls and the tween audience, meanwhile, our shows extend from *Good Luck Charlie* – a firm family favourite featuring global superstar Bridgit Mendler – to one of our newest additions, *Liv and Maddie*, starring upcoming talent Dove Cameron, who is also in the Disney Channel original movie, *Cloud 9*. Then there's our hit sitcom *Jessie,* which recently helped Disney Channel secure the BAFTA Kids' Vote for the sixth consecutive year in 2013.

A core theme of these shows for older children is celebrating family and friendship. And building on hits such as *Good Luck Charlie* with new teen sitcoms like *I Didn't Do It* and the forthcoming *Girl Meets World*, has helped Disney Channel retain its position as the UK's number one pay-TV kids channel in pay-TV homes for the eighth year running.

We are immensely proud of such successes, but never complacent. Hit shows don't come about by chance: they are born of a creative culture driven by a desire to find the strongest stories and storytelling talent and a commitment to listening to our audience.

Local programming plays an important role in our search for the best stories and storytelling; we co-ordinate this through our European production team. Providing access to a worldwide audience is a great way to foster European talent. Disney Junior's *Henry Hugglemonster*, a series about a family of loveable monsters produced in Dublin by Brown Bag Films, is a good example of this. Then there's *Evermoor* – Disney Channel's forthcoming live action mystery comedy – which is being made by Liverpool-based Lime Pictures. Both are powerful illustrations of how local production widens children's access to a broader array of narrative styles. And when it launches, *Evermoor* will be the first UK-made, long-form, live-action drama to air on Disney Channel in the US – a fantastic achievement for all the team working on the show.

from left to right Goalmouth, Gravity Falls, Star Wars Rebels

Other local productions are breaking new ground with the stories they tell. Bristol-based ArthurCox's new series, *Nina Needs to Go*, is about a preschooler who needs the bathroom at the most inopportune moments. *Goalmouth* is the only dedicated football entertainment show for kids in the UK, and with *Aim High* we offer children inspirational mentorships and a once in a lifetime experience in their chosen field.

Listening to our audience involves using a wide array of research including regular focus groups, brand trackers and audience insight for each of our channels and all of our programmes. And this helps shape the content we create and the nature of our service.

Disney Junior audience feedback highlighted a desire to feature children's precious moments, so we came up with *Birthday Book,* which is a daily celebration for little ones, and *Snuggletime,* an opportunity at bedtime for parents to share an important moment in the day with their child. Feedback also showed that there was an appetite for further genres on Disney Channel, so we looked to brilliant game show *Win, Lose or Draw,* which launched this year. And our recent realignment of Disney XD as the place for hilarious, outrageous, unpredictable fun, led to us creating 'Steve the Llama' an on-air, back to school promotion and navigation character, which beat stiff competition from BBC and Sky to win Disney XD a Promax Gold for Best Campaign last year.

Our strategy of showcasing major new shows online ahead of their TV premiere is informed by on-going research into how non-linear, on-demand, and catch-up services are altering the younger audience's viewing patterns. A recent example of this was *Austin & Ally*, which drove record numbers to tune in online.

Responding to an audience's wants and needs goes hand-in-hand with a desire to innovate. It has to – given the central role digital media now plays in young children's daily lives. Another wonderful aspect of my job is Disney's focus on pushing the creative boundaries with the stories we tell, extending those stories beyond the confines of linear TV, and enabling our viewers to actively participate in, contribute to and share these interactive experiences in new and unexpected ways.

Our many recent innovations include second screen events around event launches and special moments such as *Teen Beach Movie*, or enabling kids to send in personal messages to be seen on-screen on Valentine's Day. As well as long-form content for our TV channels and on-demand services, we develop short-form content to meet the growing demand for online consumption on our websites, YouTube channels and Facebook pages. We actively use digital platforms to engage with our audience directly, regularly running competitions and polls. And apps like the 'Disney Junior's Appisodes' enable our audiences to interact more closely with our characters, stories and each other. Meanwhile, our 'Disney Channel Photo Finish' app enables kids to personalise their pictures with favourite Disney characters and even features audio recognition software that releases bonus content when it 'hears' the user watching their favourite Disney Channel show.

Our mission is to build emotional connections and the immersive content and amazing experiences we are creating introduce the next generation to iconic characters and beautiful stories, old and new. As TV has become one of the Disney brand's most powerful ambassadors, I can't think of a more exciting place to be.

In at the Deep End 06
Multi-tasking at Beakus Animation Studio

Steve Smith

No one said it would be easy… literally no one. Everyone wants to make preschool animation, and everyone has 'an idea'. It's a crowded market, and not everyone can be *Peppa Pig*. The landscape is changing. It's fragmented, diverse, and made still more complex by new technologies and platforms. It's all about money, but no one's got any… It's about metrics, hits, downloads, shelf space, USPs, merch, pink, blue, half-hours, apps, second-third-fourth(?!)-screens… To be honest, it's kind of baffling.

But the potential to reach out to a children's audience and show them something amazing, magical, captivating, enriching, and above all helpful to their lives is incredibly alluring: which is why I jumped in with both feet and started making animation for kids. However – it has been anything but easy.

I run Beakus, an animation studio based in central London, and I've been making animation of all kinds for over a decade. We crew up and down depending on the work that comes in, meaning the studio can be hellishly busy, or stupidly quiet. And my role navigates between being a producer, a director, an animator, a creative director, a rep, a technician, an accountant, and a salesman.

As a studio our output is incredibly diverse. In the past year we've made hand-drawn 2D animation; high-spec 3D CGI; projection mapping; interactive games; corporate videos; large-scale gallery projections; infographic and character-driven narratives; even a little stop motion. We're a classic studio set-up, in that we exclusively represent a set of directors who bring their considerable animation and storytelling skills to the table, in return for committed promotion and a kind of paternal nurturing from Beakus. We're a studio of filmmakers at heart, and, in all of this, the common thread is our studio ethos: that animation is amazing, and, if used well, is really the best way of conveying messages to people.

Case in point: last year we made *The Hungry Corpse*, a dark, nine-minute, CGI short, funded by the photographer Rankin through his 'Collabor8te' scheme. I say funded, but really the money only covered a tenth of the actual budget. But raising any money for a short film these days is still cause for celebration! It was a huge undertaking that relied on the goodwill of a host of talented freelancers dropping in when they could; the long-term commitment of director Gergely Wootsch; and considerable resources 'donated' by Beakus itself. However, the film has been incredibly well received at festivals around the world, no doubt due in part to the contribution of Bill Nighy's gravelly voice and Gergely's beautifully textured design work. On the flip side we also made the titles to Sue Perkins's comedy series *Heading*

Out. Traditionally animated by hand, albeit in Flash, and artworked in Photoshop, the thirty-second sequence took two weeks to make, so breezed through the studio in the blink of an eye!

So Beakus services an industry of diverse clients, from large corporates like Google to agencies like McCann Erickson; broadcasters like the BBC; museums like the National Maritime Museum: all companies who *need* animation, and have a procurement method to go get it. For our part, we have to ensure we're in the right place at the right time, at the right budget, with the right skill and talent. But the deal is they give you some money in return for your artistry. They go off with your work and exploit it, whilst you go fishing for the next client, wiser, slightly richer, but with nothing to actually call your own.

That's another reason why the world of children's television is so attractive to me, as it must be to so many other creatives and producers who want to own something they make (yes, I know, you'll never actually own it all, but a small slice of something is better than a small slice of nothing, right?). Another reason, if I needed one, is that it just so happens I also became a dad a few years ago, which put children's TV literally front and centre... Oh, and another reason, if one were needed, is that my wife, Leigh Hodgkinson, makes picture books... So I wasn't short of inspiration!

Running a busy animation studio doesn't leave much time to sit down and develop original IP, so I took some baby steps in to the brightly coloured world of children's media by working with CBeebies on their own show, *Numtums*, taking it from development through to production of the first series (25 x 5 minutes), all made in-house at Beakus. Did I make that sound easy? Well, of course I didn't just stroll in to CBeebies and come away with a series to make: we'd pitched designs for other development series and created work for CBBC and CBeebies Presentation before on a studio-for-hire basis, so we were a known quantity. Animating a whole series is another thing altogether though. However, having that decade of commercial production behind me meant I could answer all the questions CBeebies posed, and in reality working through a series was not all that different to commercials after all. Just stretched out...

Needless to say, we had to sign all our creative work straight over to the Beeb, but we knew it would happen right from the outset, and the experience was still a thrill and a pleasure – and a perfect opportunity to learn about TV series. *Numtums* lit two sparks inside me as emails flooded in from parents asking when we'd be making the plush toys: "Wow! Kids love this!" and "Damn! I wish I could sell them plush toys..." But it wasn't my IP to sell.

So I decided to work on our studio's first IP. An opportunity arose to develop a series from some amazing, unique children's songs a friend had written but didn't know what to do with. We made a pilot and developed the concept – the costs bore equally between myself and the composer – and I threw myself in to finding a broadcaster. Oh if only I knew what I know now... Hell, does that take

time! Unpaid time… Dedicated time… Research, travel, conferences, meetings, chitchat, development, rewrites, bibles, tests and pilots… all on a wing and a prayer, and all whilst continuing my day job with fast turnaround commercial projects. I see now why it's *like* having a child. I put *like* in italics because of course it's nothing like having a child, except perhaps that IP development also needs constant attention, room to grow, and heaps of financial investment. Thankfully it doesn't fill a nappy…

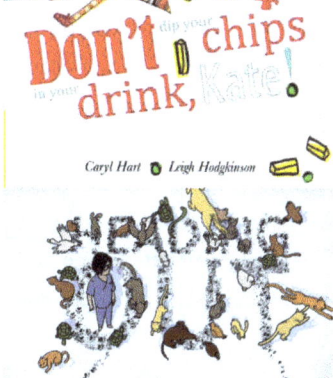

I gave up on that IP a year later. That's not very long, I discover, to lug a project around, but despite vacillating between shouts of, "It's happening!" and, "It's shelved!" I became wary of investing all my efforts in to a song-driven show where the creative team had differing expectations. I had also become classically disillusioned having been led on a merry dance by someone much bigger who wanted to 'develop' the project with us but, it turned out, take complete ownership in the process. You've got to have your wits about you – there are sharks in these here waters…

In the meantime, *Numtums* series 2 came along. It was going to be a lot bigger, a lot more costly. The tender went out a few months before the UK tax breaks were expected to arrive on the scene and, despite plunging in to the world of co-pros, we couldn't make the money work – our tender got thrown out for having to rely on the tax breaks. As a small studio, creatively-led, we just couldn't source enough money to take on the show, and an opportunity went begging. *Numtums* series 2 has aired now, and it still makes use of the original character designs we gave away back in 2011, so for me it was a chastening experience and an important reminder that money really does move this world.

Dusting myself off, I began work on a new IP, inspired by my wife's workshops with children about her books. We're now eighteen months on, and we've designed and written about the world of *Toggle* in great depth. We made a teaser that got me to MIP Junior where I took part in the International Pitch (and lost to a yogic cow. A *yogic cow*!!) and then received a pre-buy from CBeebies (very proud of that).

When CBeebies said "YES!" most industry types I talked to smiled back telling me I was practically home and dry. I went to distributors who told me they love it but don't do advances anymore (not like in the *old days*). I got channels interested in pre-buys but was warned if I took channel 'X' I wouldn't be able to get channel 'Y'. I discovered quickly that French broadcasters aren't legally allowed to take shows aimed at lower preschool... And we got rejected from Cartoon Forum despite endorsement from CBeebies. The list goes on: tick that box, cross that one…

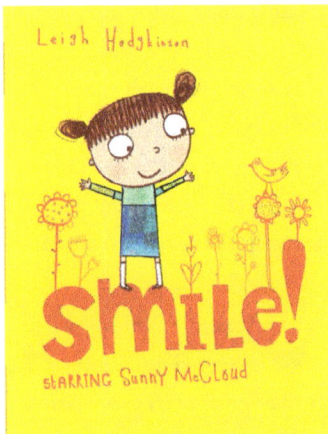

Other interested broadcasters gave a standard 'delaying' response: they needed to see a full ep. So we made a full length pilot that children love (according to CBeebies focus groups, not me, you cynic). It was worth the investment just to explore the world, story, voices, music and style of *Toggle*, and I've been excited to show it to broadcasters – experiencing Kidscreen for the first time earlier this year. We now have a distributor, a certificate that guarantees the UK tax breaks, a roster of ten international broadcasters, and a successful Creative Europe Media Fund application! We're not there yet, of course, but progress is progress!

Every hurdle that suddenly presents itself along this journey is just another lesson on how our industry works. If it were easy we'd all be doing it – heck, we all are, but with greater or lesser success. I'm amazed anyone traverses this minefield, and doff my hat to those who have (especially those who come back for more). As well as learning how to be a 'showrunner', all I really want to do is make great animation for children; tell stories; make them laugh and learn; and marvel at how clever animation can be. There's no way I could pursue a series concept this long and far without being totally committed and confident it'll amaze our audience.

Everyone I meet with IP under their arms will say the same thing, but hopefully we're not all delusional! I speak at universities and often meet students who are busy developing their own IP, convinced it's better than anything out there. I hate myself for throwing water on their kindling embers – telling them it takes a long, long time to get something off the ground so, maybe, like, get a job too? – but there's no way around it. Ideas take time to gestate and find a perfect home. They take committed time and energy to find that home. And doing that whilst holding down a job is really tough. But then, no one said it was going to be easy.

　　　　　top to bottom Leo and the Lift, Limelight Larry, Smile!

People sometimes ask me what it's like writing for kids, and how do I get my head around writing in a particular way. I know what they're getting at but, at the same time, I don't quite understand the question. For me, writing for kids is exactly the same as writing for adults. It's all about telling a good story, and you've got to do it well. The only difference is tone, and often there is very little distinguishable between the tone of a kids' show versus what happens in primetime (comedy, in particular).

In many ways, writing for kids is the purest form of storytelling because it's free of ego and cynicism. Kids don't care if you're Russell T. Davies. They only care if Russell T. Davies tells them a good story. An idea that grabs. A story with a sense of urgency. Characters that we really care about. A plot with unpredictable twists and turns. Think kids aren't sophisticated and can't see a twist from a mile away? Think again. But apart from quality storytelling, another prerequisite for children's TV is the ability to write a funny script. No postmodern cultural references, intellectual quips or self-reflexive wit: just make the script funny through the characters and story. No pressure.

The number one rule about writing for children's television is: never be patronizing to your audience. Kids are far smarter than their parents, especially when it comes to story! Another good consideration is that stories should be childlike rather than childish. Childlike means having that sense of fun, curiosity and optimism about the world. Childish antics have their place (as many characters might have a childish outlook) but silly and stupid behaviour just for the sake of it doesn't do anybody any favours.

Kids' TV breaks down into a number of different categories: drama, factual, animation, light entertainment and preschool (and comedy runs through the heart of each category). Preschool targets children up to age four: colourful worlds and characters specific to positive child development (e.g. *Teletubbies*). Drama and animation for four to twelve year olds gets broken down into subcategories of target age groups: four to six, six to nine, and nine to twelve year olds. Six to nine year olds is the sweet spot for most programmes. Shows targeted for nine to twelve year olds will typically be more ambitious and adventure-led, like *The Sarah Jane Adventures* and *Leonardo*.

How do you get the opportunity to write for kids' TV? Well, it's the same process as primetime drama or feature films. You need to have written a spec script, and preferably a spec script in the kids' TV genre. Formats for kids' TV tend to be shorter (e.g. eleven-minute episodes), so a fifteen page spec script would suffice (especially if it's backed up with a series bible that expands and illustrates the world of the story).

Then you target the relevant producers and production companies that are making kids' TV shows. If your query/approach lands at the right time and place, and they like your work, you may very well find yourself pitching for a commission on a show they have already in the works (there is a chance they might want to option your spec submission but an opportunity to pitch for their existing show is more likely). Pitching for a commission means that the producers are willing to receive ideas from you as potential episodes of their show. You don't (typically) get paid for this. The pitches are usually a paragraph long, rarely more than a page. If the idea is accepted, then you'll be commissioned to script, with the usual outline and scene-by-scene stages in between. Occasionally, you may be invited to 'writer workshops' (and receive a modest attendance fee) where a number of writers will meet to discuss the series (the tone, characters, rules etc.), and after that, you'll be asked to submit ideas. But just because you've attended the workshop, there's no guarantee of a commission unless the idea is really good.

Over there on the Twitter, that you have nowadays, I asked some lovely TV folk to share their tips and advice on writing for children. A lot of it chimed with the above but here's a selection of replies:

Phil Ford, writer of *The Sarah Jane Adventures* and *Wizards vs Aliens* (with Russell T. Davies) said: "If you think of a story you don't think you could write for kids, write it! The best kids' TV challenges its audience, and most of all challenges the writer. Writing good kids' TV is tough work!"

Debbie Moon, creator/writer of *Wolfblood* for CBBC: "Remember you're writing for a broad age range. Kids' TV is often defined as 8-12s but there could be much younger siblings in the room. Kids have specific concerns: family, friendship, loyalty, fitting in. Boyfriend/girlfriend relationships not a big concern. Oh, and you can't kill human beings. Aliens are OK but no humans (one of the few drawbacks to writing for kids!)."

James Henry (*Bob the Builder*): "If it's the preschool demographic, try not to give any character dialogue that runs for more than two lines. Try to have problems solved with a nice visual/action rather than characters just talking to each other."

Mark Huckerby & Nick Ostler, BAFTA winners, *The Amazing Adrenalini Brothers*: "Kids' shows eat up stories. 52 eps is not unusual. Schedules are brutal. Be the head writer's friend by being a problem solver ... take notes well: they might seem silly but there's usually a good reason for them. Write fast, but don't be sloppy ... be prolific with ideas, but be prepared to dig deep for original ones; don't submit first thoughts, they'll be clichés. Don't assume because it's for kids that the storytelling standards should be any lower!"

So writing for kids' TV is a real skill yet, speaking from personal experience, it's created a little confusion for a handful of execs I've met over the years: "OK, you've written for the soaps, done some horror, but also live-action and animation kids' shows. Trouble is, we don't know what kind of writer you are." I know what they're getting at but, at the same time, I don't quite understand the confusion. I like to think I'm a versatile writer who has talents across many genres and formats but it seems TV (and film) likes to know, specifically, what kind of writer you are so they know where they can put you. Fair enough, I guess, but it can be frustrating at times.

Still, this frustration led to a rethink on my part. How should I present myself to the industry? What kind of writer do I ultimately want to be, or to be known for? A really useful conversation with my agent nailed it: "If you find yourself getting work in one area, and really enjoy it, then don't fight it, focus on that as much as possible." And I thought to myself: yeah, I'm proud to call myself a children's writer. Why not take the ambiguity away, and concentrate on what gives me a lot of enjoyment but also the most regular work? It was just a slight shift of viewpoint on my part but it snapped into focus my immediate ambitions.

Ever since I've embraced my proud 'writer for kids' POV, the work has flowed with more regularity, and a better consistency has emerged on my CV. And this year, I'm taking it even further. I'm writing and directing a live-action children's film: a mystery adventure that's exclusively for kids with kids in the lead roles (and an original idea to boot. Sssh, it's not based on a pre-existing intellectual property!). It's called *Who Killed Nelson Nutmeg?* and if you'd like to know more (or even get involved or support the project) you can see my details in the 'Contributors' section at the back of this book.

LIMA UK
The Good News About Licensing
Kelvyn Gardner

08

For as long as there has been children's media in any form, there has been licensing based on that media. For example, one widely known story is that of the mother of Jeremy Clarkson, Shirley, who started making and selling *Paddington Bear* plush toys in the early 1970s. She was not aware of the rights issues, but eventually was granted an official licence, the first company to gain this status in the UK. This story is by no means the oldest (we can go back to Mickey Mouse and Ingersoll watches for this), but I quote it as the medium concerned was not TV, film or even radio, but books.

To explain a little more, licensing is the process by which manufacturers and marketers of consumer goods and services obtain permission (a licence) to produce goods utilising third party intellectual property. Thus products as diverse as toys and games, digital apps, home furnishings, stationery, gifts, toiletries – you name it – can be produced under licence. The manufacturer pays for the rights by way of a royalty on each item sold. In my own career, the most unusual licence in which I was involved was when I arranged a deal between a small theatrical production company and Fremantle Media to produce a live version of *Family Fortunes* that ran in Butlins in the summer of 2003. Nowadays one of my roles is to head up the UK branch of the international trade association for licensing, LIMA (Licensing Industry Merchandisers Association). LIMA seeks to promote the wider use of licensing as a marketing tool both nationally and across the world, and in these efforts we are therefore umbilically connected to the media world (for children, yes, but for adults too), with the licensing of brands, films and drama like *Game of Thrones* or *Downton Abbey*.

Given that licensing revenues are now so important to the children's media business (more on this below), LIMA's task here is of high importance. Although licensing is an established business sector, with retail sales in the UK in the billions of pounds, it is still not a business process much understood by British industry as a whole. Consumer goods companies very often simply don't know where to start. They may hear from friends and family that a certain TV show is popular with youngsters, but they do not see the framework that exists to connect a manufacturer to that show.

That's not to say that licensing has always been wholly embraced by all aspects of children's media. In my early days in the industry, at the beginning of the 1980s, in the UK at least there was little direct contact, for instance, between TV programme makers and broadcasters on the one hand and licensing-based businesses on the other. There was clearly a reluctance on the part of the former to 'get their hands dirty', by dealing with me and my peers. We were regarded as strictly commercial exploiters of this media, whereas the TV folk were creative artists who should positively avoid having a hand in such activity. There's no denying that licensing does 'exploit', in a non-pejorative sense, the appeal, fame and desirability of children's media to sell products. But, step back for a moment, and realise that much TV is funded by advertising – hardly less commercial than licensing – and you can see the unfairness of licensing being negatively branded as such.

Of course, there can be a genuine fear among TV producers/writers that a show might be considerably affected by licensing considerations during the creative process. I doubt what I say here will entirely calm such fears, but my experience is that, when it comes to children, licensing success only flows from high quality, imaginative programming, well-written with the programme makers' craft at the core. Attempt to 'build in' licensing success and you're likely to fail. As an example from Hollywood, in devising characters for *Star Wars* Episode One (the first of the 'prequels' released at the end of the last century), Lucasfilm created an alien with the clear intent to make this one an absolute fan favourite. At the same time, they had little faith that the villain of the film would set the franchise's fans alight, and so killed him off at the end. The net result was that fans hated the former (Jar Jar Binks) but loved the latter (Darth Maul) – exactly the opposite outcome to that anticipated by the filmmakers. If such experienced practitioners of licensing as Lucasfilm can get this wrong, what hope for the typical children's TV producer?

In fact, sometimes there's a temptation to 'improve' on a character after it has reached the public domain. Disney attracted controversy last year with regard to the heroine of the animated movie, *Brave*. In the film, Princess Merida appeared to be a female truly plucked from thistle and heather, as she had a rugged, redheaded prettiness rather than the sort of chocolate-box beauty often associated with cartoon queens-to-be. Now, it's true that Disney occasionally updates the look of their entire Princess line-up, rather in the way that football teams update their playing strip; the 'new' Merida is slimmer, and more fashion model in look than her original, despite the fact that numerous licensed products, including toys, have already enjoyed solid success based on the appearance and demeanour of the Scottish princess as she appears in the movie. Once again though, Merida's success was won by offering kids a fascinating character in a well-written storyline.

Much has happened since the 1980s on both sides of this debate. Licensing has gained in popularity and in consumer acceptance; whilst media producers have found ways to gently tweak content to allow a chance of licensing success without radically compromising their creative ideals. As we know all too well, the ever decreasing broadcaster budgets for the creation of new kids' TV has also seen programme makers more readily embrace licensing as a source of funding. The wider media, including news and current affairs output, has, little by little, come to be more positive about the role that licensing can play in the prosperity of 'UK plc'. Old favourites like *Dennis the Menace*, *Thomas the Tank Engine and Friends*, *Winnie the Pooh* and others have always held a special place in the minds of many British adults, including journalists. Accordingly, stories related to the commercial success of these creations, including licensing success, have made their way into mainstream news features.

What has taken longer is an acceptance that new creations, for TV or film, should be treated similarly. There's still a sense that if a new TV show for kids becomes popular quickly, and if merchandise goes on sale as a result, then there must be something 'exploitative' (this time most definitely in a derogatory sense) about the core endeavour. Characters, like popular musicians and actors, are also often described as 'overnight successes', heightening the idea that instant fame and fortune can be yours through little effort if you can get your show on the air. However, just like the band that slaves away in tiny clubs for years before finally breaking through, nothing can be further from the truth in most (licensing) cases. *Teletubbies* may have risen very swiftly in its day, but it was on the back of years of hard work, and learning, by Anne Wood and Andrew Davenport. The creators of *Pokémon* spent seven years trying to get their idea into the hands of a powerful media company before it came to the public's attention.

Thankfully, even this attitude is changing. The success in the last ten years of *Peppa Pig* is a great illustration. Peppa is rightly regarded as an excellent piece of children's animation. In theme, it breaks a lot of 'normal success rules' notably in having a family of pigs (not normally considered the most child- or merchandise-friendly animals) as the stars of the show. The writing is engaging and amusing, even for daddy and mummy pigs (try the 'United Nations' episode, my favourite). Although the principal star is female, Daddy Pig and George help draw interest from boys. In 2012 Peppa broke through the £200 million barrier of annual retail sales of merchandise, with high levels of exports of both the show and the licensing. All the national newspapers covered this success, as did much of TV and radio. Even I was interviewed by *BBC Radio 5 Live* on the topic.

How refreshing then to see licensing success celebrated as a good news story for 'UK plc'. Handled rightly, licensing can grow its hard-fought status as a true ally of children's media, helping fund projects and companies who are trying to bring exciting new projects – TV, Web, App, even radio – to audiences of children here and around the world, and bringing excitement and fun itself through the opportunity to enjoy play with media characters in the everyday environment.

The British Toy and Hobby Association
Natasha Crookes

09

The British Toy and Hobby Association (BTHA) works to promote best practice and excellence in all aspects of product design, toy safety, ethical manufacturing, environmental affairs and responsible marketing and by so doing aims to protect and promote the interests of members. This encompasses a range of services and campaigns to members and the wider community, including organizing the annual toy industry trade fair: The Toy Fair®. The association will celebrate its 70th anniversary in 2014.

The BTHA, and its membership, support and run the consumer focused 'Make Time 2 Play' campaign. Play is an important part of child development, helping children to learn the skills they will need in later life. Toys can act as the tools that help children to learn, increasing the time that children spend playing and acting as a catalyst to promote different types of play. Children should have a balanced play diet to help them develop as wide a range of skills as possible with a little of different types of play scattered throughout the day and the week. The Make Time 2 Play campaign aims to explain the many benefits that play has, whilst children are simply having fun. It also gives parents play ideas to fill playtime easily and to encourage a diversity of play experiences. The campaign has been running since 2010 and has a Facebook page, website and app. Children's media television channels and cinema support the campaign by running adverts directing parents to play resources. The campaign would not be possible without the support of Five/Milkshake, Sky Kids, ITVBe, Turner, Disney XD and Disney Junior, Tiny Pop and Digital Cinema Media (DCM).

Members of the British Toy and Hobby Association see themselves and their products within this important context and take seriously their responsibility to make quality toys that can help children to develop the skills they need whilst having lots of fun. Quality toys need to go through a long process (18-24 months) of development before they reach the shelf for customers to buy. Development starts with initial research into trends and sales, examination of play patterns and children's preferences, and takes into consideration incredibly strict safety legislation including choice of materials, safe design, age range grading and the play interests of the audience/consumer. BTHA members' first priority is toy safety and the BTHA works with members, UK and EU government and UK authorities such as Trading Standards to ensure that the products of our members are safe and enjoyable to play with.

Even after all the research and development that goes into a toy it is notoriously difficult to predict what will be the big hit of the year. Often that will be decided in playgrounds around the country when children come back from their summer holidays and start to talk about the television and films they have seen; the toys they have played with; activities they have taken part in; and what is new and exciting. It takes experience and knowledge for retailers to be able to pick, from the tens of thousands of new toys on the market each year, the ones they think children will like best.

Last year the toy industry in the UK was worth £2.9 billion: a decline of one per cent in value. About a quarter of toys were linked with a character from a movie, TV show or game licence. Pocket money toys declined most overall, as main presents were still being bought for birthdays and Christmas but fewer low-priced purchases were made throughout the year: this is thought to be due to a squeeze on consumer spending.

The bright spots in 2013 were toys in the 'Youth electronics' and 'Games & puzzles' categories. Furby experienced a 66 per cent increase in sales compared to 2012, and was the bestselling toy for the year. Other strong performers included Barbie, Playmobil, The Ninja Turtles, LEGO and LEGO Friends. Strong performers for preschool properties were *Peppa Pig*, *Mickey & Friends*, Little Tikes and *Doc McStuffins*.

The toy sector is fast moving and innovative – launching thousands of new products to market every year – and 2014 is predicted to regain the loss seen in 2013 with the launch of new and exciting toys. Growth is expected to be particularly strong within the 'Building sets' and 'Action figure' sectors, with a ten per cent increase predicted for the latter. The growth in 2014 will be propelled by four main factors: movies, the FIFA World Cup, technology toys, and pocket money toys.

In 2014 the BTHA will focus on its priorities for the industry, continuing to ensure safe toys reach the market whilst continuing ongoing work in the areas of ethical manufacturing, environmental projects and responsible marketing. Members of the BTHA sign up to the ICTI CARE code of business practices to monitor the working conditions of toy factories. The BTHA has a sustainability committee that oversees work in this important area of business and gives advice and guidance to members to encourage continuous development on sustainable and environmental affairs.

The BTHA also advocates for responsible marketing to children and their families. All BTHA members sign an annual code of practice, which commits them to promoting their toys in a decent, honest and truthful manner, to abide by advertising codes, and, where a form of marketing has not yet been covered by legislation, to apply the spirit of the existing codes. BTHA members sign annually the Advertising Association's pledge of peer-to-peer marketing and the BTHA has guidelines for members on responsible marketing practices. In addition the BTHA was a founding, and continuous supporting member, of Media Smart – the school media literacy campaign.

The BTHA administers the toy industry charity, the Toy Trust, which has raised more than £3 million for children's charities. Each year media companies give advertising slots for catalogues and television that are auctioned to the toy industry to raise money. These funds, along with those raised at fundraising events throughout the year, are disbursed to children's charities to help disadvantaged children. The Toy Trust gave money to more than 70 children's charities in 2013, amounting to grants totaling more than a quarter of a million pounds.

The BTHA and its members believe in promoting play in all its forms to help children develop the skills they need for life. There is no wrong type of play as long as children are safe. The BTHA has help and guidance on a multitude of matters affecting children and their families which can be found on our website or on the Make Time 2 Play website: full details are given in the 'Contributors' section at the back of this book.

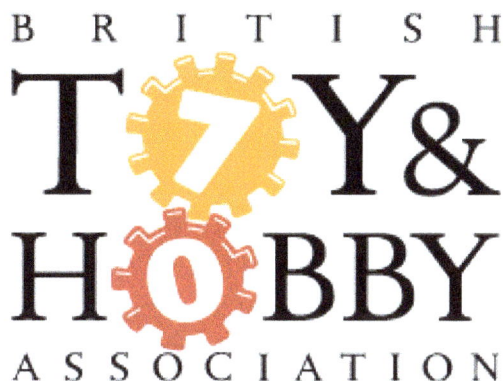

Gender Skewing in Children's Media   10
Julia Posen

Walker Books is a leading independent children's publisher and IP owner, renowned for our original content and outstanding quality. As well as publishing many award-winning authors, illustrators, titles and brands, we also have an in-house licensing division to manage activity across some of those brands including *Maisy* and all other properties by Lucy Cousins: *Guess How Much I Love You* and *Tilly and Friends*. And we have an in-house independent production company, Walker Productions, to develop Walker content for TV with projects including *Tilly and Friends* for CBeebies, *Henry Hugglemonster* for Disney, *Fleabag Monkeyface* for CITV and, most recently, the new live-action series *Hank Zipzer*, starring Henry 'The Fonz' Winkler, for CBBC.

Ultimately, creativity is at the heart of everything we do, and we are always looking for ways to take our content to as many children as possible. We do encounter issues of gender skews and stereotyping within our publishing, licensing and TV production work and our approach to them and the controls we do and don't have varies across the different arms of the business.

To address publishing first, which accounts for the lion's share of what we do, we publish a diverse range of titles aimed at every age group: from picture books to young adult (YA) fiction. Our primary considerations for acquisition are quality, content and age-appropriateness. While gender is certainly something we think about, it is not a consideration that drives content or design. However, the role of gender in the purchaser's decision-making does alter subtly across the different age groups.

To start with preschool, at this age we find that our publishing brands appeal almost equally to boys and girls. We know that boys as well as girls enjoy *Tilly and Friends* and *Maisy* in spite of the female names in the title. Both Tilly and Maisy represent childhood – imagination, play, discovery, friendships – universal themes. And *We're Going on a Bear Hunt* and *Guess How Much I Love You* have both been enjoyed by boys and girls for more than twenty years. You can see from our covers that we favour a gender neutral approach, using strong design and colour palettes aimed at appealing to a wide audience.

As we reach the mid-age range, the six plus category, we find a slightly piqued interest in books specifically for girls and books specifically for boys. Interestingly this is also where self-purchase begins to kick in, meaning that children of this age begin to actively request favoured titles or brands rather than simply receiving books as gifts from adult family members and friends. But this by no means dictates our publishing strategy in this area. We continue to provide a broad range of titles for all of our readers. Series like Vivian French's *Stargirl Academy* has skewed more to a girl audience, and Tommy Donbavand's *Fangs Vampire Spy* has done well with boys. Popular series like *Where's Wally?* continue to perform brilliantly for both boys and girls, as does *Hank Zipzer*, which is now proving equally popular on the CBBC channel.

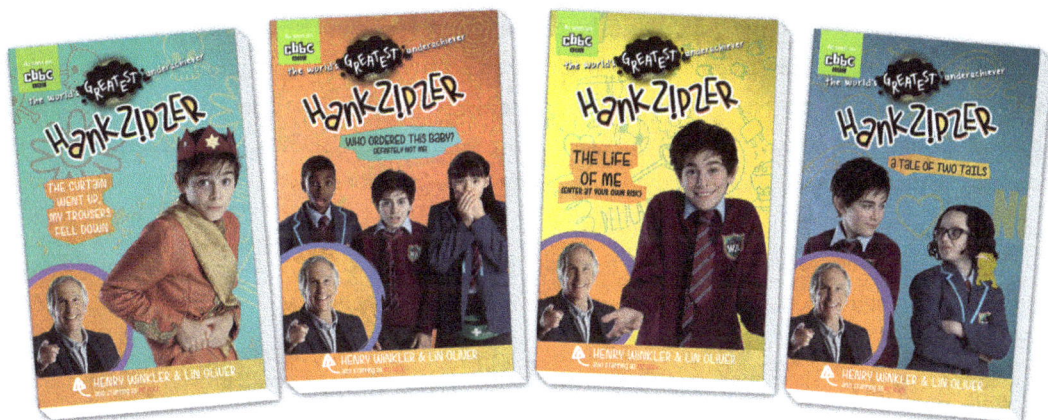

From a commercial point of view, targeting one gender can slightly reduce risk in a project in that you can focus on one audience and narrow the approach. But, in reality, we try to appeal to a wider, mixed audience. This is partly because we believe that even series we know to be predominantly enjoyed by boys – *Alex Rider* for instance, a series universally acclaimed for bringing more boys to reading – still appeals to many girls, with plenty of them writing reader reviews, taking part in competitions and turning up to signings and events.

Our marketing strategy reflects this view, and within the mid-range age group we mainly work with gender neutral magazines and third-party partners such as National Geographic Kids, First News, Bin Weevils and Swapit, all of whom have a fairly even girl/boy split.

Moving on to our YA publishing, Patrick Ness has won every major book award going in the last couple of years for his novels. He appeals to both male and female readers and the content of his brilliant stories reflects this, the same can be said of Mal Peet. Cassandra Claire, author of the *Mortal Instruments* trilogy, has found her core fan base amongst girls, much like the *Twilight* series, but this doesn't mean we put pink on the cover of each one!

Significantly for us, most book retailers shelve books by age group rather than boy/girl sections and that too helps us steer away from gender skewing. In our experience of selling to library and educational markets, we find a similar absence of gender differentiation. Also, as digital publishing continues to take hold, packaging is stripped back even further – reading on a Kindle or similar electronic device often means readers are presented purely with content, without any kind of cover design or packaging at all.

It is also very gratifying to see the headlines this week proclaiming the effectiveness of the 'Let Books Be Books' campaign (of which you can read more in Alex Lewis Paul's article in the 'Commentary and Debate' section of this yearbook), which have included the *Independent on Sunday* pledging to no longer review gender stereotyped children's titles and both Parragon and Usborne declaring they will no longer publish them. This campaign has drawn vocal support from Waterstones and several high profile children's authors. It has successfully brought the issue into the public spotlight, with two of our own authors, Anthony Horowitz and Bel Mooney, appearing on the *BBC One Breakfast Show* and Radio 4's *Today* programme respectively to offer their support for these initiatives.

To conclude, the 'sweet spot' for publishers is gender neutral, and in the last couple of years we've seen that the best commercial opportunities lie here. Jeff Kinney's *Diary of a Wimpy Kid*; the novels of David Walliams and of Michael Morpurgo; and Julia Donaldson's picture books are all fine examples of this. It is content that drives the publishing industry so I think that can give us comparatively more creative freedom when it comes to presenting titles to consumers and allows us to take an inclusive approach.

Considering next our licensing activity, Walker is at its heart a children's publishing company, but as the industry started to expand and shift we could see new opportunities become available to us and our authors and illustrators. Walker has always had a small licensing operation, mostly managed by external agents, but in the last three years we have grown it significantly, bringing the majority of activity in-house and expanding our licensing division. All of our current brands are preschool: *Maisy*, *Guess How Much I Love You*, *We're Going on a Bear Hunt* and *Tilly and Friends*.

Our licensing business involves different processes to our publishing business, although we are still ultimately targeting the same end-consumers. We are responsible for creating the style guides for our brands, and we work closely with our licensees and retailers to ensure we're delivering product and designs that remain true to the brand while appealing as widely as possible. All our style guides include a gender neutral creative direction, but there are occasions when licensees and retailers specifically request a more targeted direction aimed at girls or boys, as a result of their consumer demand.

The key driving categories for our licensing business, bringing in 80 per cent of our revenue, are: toys and games, publishing, DVD, apparel, gifts and stationery. When it comes to gender, licensing reflects publishing in the preschool categories and the approach tends to be gender neutral in terms of toys, DVD and gifts. Just as we see in publishing, licensed product for preschool is also driven by parent and gift-purchase rather than self-purchase.

Interestingly though, even in the preschool market, apparel categories are already being approached differently in terms of gender skew. There are reasons for this, not least of all that boys and girls clothes are different. They're racked in different sections; they follow different trends and styles. When it comes to colours, it's not always as simple as just being blue for boys or pink for girls, but there does seem to be a social expectation around certain colours being more 'girly' for instance. The one retailer that was an exception to this rule was the much missed Woolworths, which stacked its product by brand rather than gender, proving that it is possible to move away from this model. There is a bookshop chain in Germany called Thalia which follows a similar approach. The excellent 'Let Toys Be Toys' campaign (from which the 'Let Books Be Books' campaign was born) has successfully convinced several UK retailers to do away with their 'boys' and 'girls' sections but there is some way to go before this becomes the norm.

Briefly taking each of these brands in turn, here are a few examples of our approach to new product lines (it is worth noting that the packaging is always kept gender neutral):

Maisy Mouse – Selling 31 million books worldwide, published in 29 languages and almost 25 years old, Maisy continues to have broad appeal. She has a girl's name, but looks like a boy! Product ranges have, over the years, included toys, games, books and gifts, all of which use the bold primary colours of Lucy Cousins and aim to appeal to both boys and girls. However in order for consumers to continue to engage with brands, style guides need to be regularly revisited and updated to keep them contemporary and fresh. One of these creative directions included adding a 'Love Maisy' strand to sit alongside existing designs, incorporating an apparel line aimed at girls with mock-ups of 'Love Maisy' on skirts and dresses. *Maisy* has extraordinary versatility as a brand, and this has been a way of demonstrating that to retailers, whilst still appealing to both boys and girls equally.

Guess How Much I Love You – We launched the *Guess…* baby and infant range last year, with apparel lines, plush toys, gifts and nursery décor. While the style guide included a gender neutral design palette, we also needed to include additional colour ways in both blue and pink for the apparel lines. With 70 per cent of the population now finding out the sex of their baby before the birth, the retail message to us, based on consumer feedback, is that pink and blue sells. There still seems to be an association in modern society with pink for girls and blue for boys, and right from the very beginning, that's what they're looking for. It is worth noting that the style guides we provide are used as design suggestions. They are not blue prints for the licensee – they will create their own suggested range for retailers' buy-in.

Tilly and Friends – this is a really interesting brand for us. Based on the picture books by Polly Dunbar, Walker Productions co-produced the animated TV series (currently airing on CBeebies) with JAM Media. The publishing programme for Tilly is very gender neutral and we know it is enjoyed by girls and boys. As we developed the style guide for *Tilly and Friends* though, we could see that the creative direction was leaning more heavily towards girls in certain categories, particularly apparel. While the stories, activities and colour palettes in the *Tilly* series aim to be gender neutral, many of the tiny design elements, the icons and motifs, are more girl-orientated. Little boys might like butterflies, and enjoy watching them, but many of them don't want to wear butterflies on their T-shirts! It's a similar situation with a competitor's brand, *Peppa Pig*, universally enjoyed by girls and boys, but when it came to the apparel line, it was the case that the licensing strategy was to build George as the character to front the boys' lines.

Tilly… poses lots of interesting questions around gender. We don't view it as a 'girls only' brand – we know little boys like it too. And we took great care to ensure that Tilly represents a number of positive, strong female role models: the female characters – Tilly, Pru and Doodle – are all very different in their personalities and views, and the very fact that Doodle is a crocodile seems to challenge most gender stereotypes where crocodiles are almost always boys!

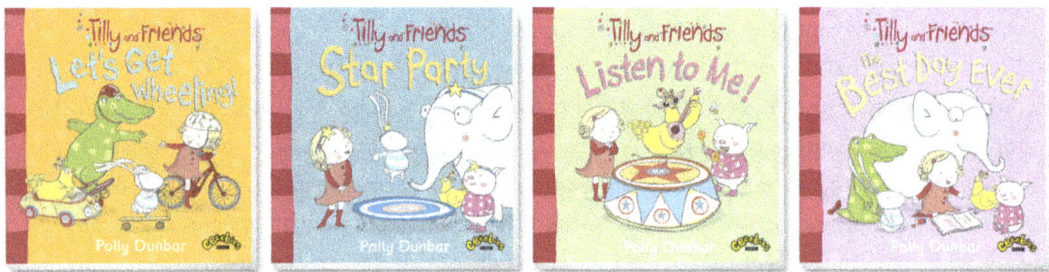

In conclusion, Walker is always trying to find new and inclusive ways of bringing our stories, brands and characters to as many children as possible. We enjoy relative creative freedom in the way we develop our brands for both publishing and licensing, but of course we observe and factor in our consumer buying habits. I believe it's important for different industries to come together to help address some of the challenges we all face around the broader social perceptions and expectations of gender in childhood.

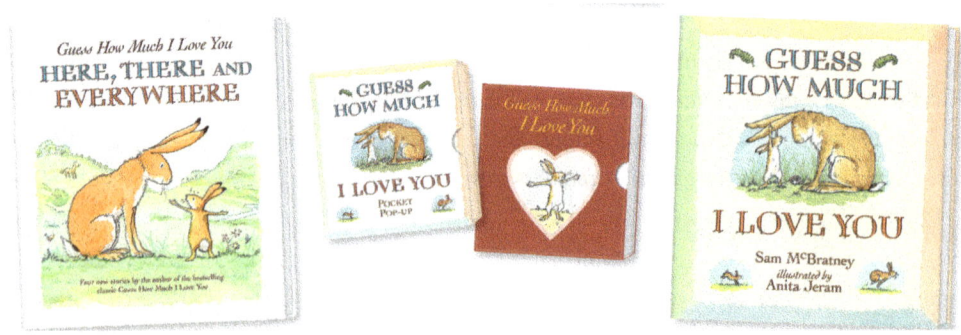

The British Board of Film Classification (11)
David Austin

The British Board of Film Classification (BBFC) is an independent, non-governmental, not for profit body which has classified cinema films since 1912 and videos/DVDs since the Video Recordings Act (VRA) was passed in 1984. Our age ratings are: U; PG; 12A for cinema releases (and 12 for video releases); 15; 18; and R18.

We also classify content for distribution online under a 'best practice' voluntary service which we set up in partnership with industry. Classifications for online content are not required by law, though many video-on-demand (VOD) platforms, such as Netflix, iTunes, BT Vision and Sainsbury's Entertainment, recognise that BBFC age ratings are useful to parents as a guide when selecting content for their family to watch. Some VOD platforms also calibrate their parental controls in line with BBFC age ratings.

More recently the BBFC also became the provider of the classification framework used by mobile phone operators to decide what content should be put behind their network filters. The framework is binary and puts content that the BBFC considers to be suitable only for adults behind filters and parental controls.

All BBFC classification decisions are made in line with the BBFC Classification Guidelines. There are two key principles, laid out in the Guidelines, under which we operate: to protect children and vulnerable adults from potentially harmful or otherwise unsuitable content; and to empower consumers, particularly parents and those with responsibility for children, to make informed viewing decisions.

The Classification Guidelines are based on large scale public consultation and expert research. We revise the Guidelines through this consultation method every four to five years. The most recent consultation was carried out from December 2012 and throughout 2013 and involved more than 10,000 people from across the UK. The research highlighted public trust in the film classification system; with 95 per cent of parents with children under fifteen saying they usually check the BBFC classification before watching a film and 89 per cent of film viewers saying they consider classification as important. Overall 92 per cent of film viewers agreed with the classification of films and videos they had seen recently.

Anyone wanting to release a film on cinema or DVD/Blu-ray release in the UK needs to make sure the film has a BBFC age rating. VOD platforms who want to use a BBFC age rating for content they make available online must also submit it for classification (DVD/Blu-ray content automatically receives a digital age rating for use online).

When a film is finished and ready to be classified, the distributor of the film submits it to us using an online submission process. The distributor includes vital information such as how long a work is, when it is due to be released in cinemas and what rating they are aiming to achieve. It is important for us to know what rating a distributor would like, even if we don't agree with it on viewing the work, it helps tells us what age group they think the film is suitable for and any changes to achieve that rating can be considered while BBFC examiners view the film.

The distributing company pays a fee for the classification of their film, DVD/Blu-ray or online content. This fee is calculated based on the length of their film. An average length film or DVD/Blu-ray would cost about £800 or so to classify, while online content of the same length would cost around £250 to classify. The system for classifying online content is not a legal requirement, and the legal requirements placed on us by the Video Recordings Act 1984, including providing evidence in court for prosecutions under this Act, do not apply, enabling us to provide a lower-cost service for rating online content.

All film, DVD/Blu-ray and online content submitted for classification is checked by our Operations team to ensure the content is complete and good enough quality for a team of Examiners to watch it. Examiners view the exact same film that people will see in the cinema on DVD/Blu-ray or online. The Operations team also draws up a schedule for the Examining team to view all the content submitted for classification each week. Films are normally classified by a team of two Examiners in our own cinema beneath our offices in London. If the film is shot on IMAX, Examiners travel to a larger IMAX screen to classify it. DVD/Blu-ray and online content is normally examined by one Examiner in their own office. Examiners write a report after every unit of content they watch, recommending a classification. They also write 'BBFCinsight' – a summary, useful particularly for parents – of how and why a cinema film was rated at any given category.

A Senior Examiner reads and approves this report and we notify the distributing company of the classification using our online system. If the distributing company accepts the classification we will publish it on our website. We also broadcast all our cinema film classification decisions via our Twitter feed (@BBFC) and publish age ratings for films classified U, PG and 12A on our website for children, www.CBBFC.co.uk.

If a film or video sits on the border between two categories or contains very complex issues, it will be examined by a second team of Examiners and normally the Director. The President and Vice-

Presidents may also examine the most complex or challenging films and videos. A distributing company might choose to make cuts or reductions to achieve the classification they'd like for their film or video. Sometimes this isn't possible, or the distributor will decide to accept the classification awarded without making any cuts. For example, in 2013, 37 per cent of films classified were given a different classification than the one requested by the distributor.

If a film or video cannot be classified, even at the 18 category, it will be refused a classification. In this case it may not be shown in a cinema (without permission from the local authority for that cinema to show it without a classification) or sold on DVD or Blu-ray. It is quite rare for a film or video to be refused a classification since at the 18 level, our Classification Guidelines state that adults should be free to choose their own entertainment, unless the material is in breach of the criminal law; has been created through the commission of a criminal offence; or the material risks harm to individuals or, through their behaviour, to society. Such material may include, for example, certain portrayals of sexual violence.

The BBFC Classification Guidelines are based on regular large scale public consultations and are revised every four to five years. In addition we also carry out expert research. Recently, research has focused on how often the public use BBFC age ratings; whether the public wants BBFC age ratings online; and how the BBFC should classify portrayals of sexual and sadistic violence. Some of our research involves young people and children.

The review of the Classification Guidelines carried out in December 2012 and throughout 2013 involved teenagers for the first time, as well as their parents. Many teenagers are avid film fans, so their views on classification are relevant. Teenagers interviewed during the Guidelines review were seemingly more relaxed than their parents about the way in which language, soft drugs and gore is portrayed in film, but they had strong views about discrimination and sadistic and sexual violence and argued that we should continue to place great importance on these issues when classifying films.

Perhaps surprisingly, 76 per cent of teenagers rated classification as important, even though they can be frustrated that an age rating may prevent them from seeing a particular film. It is clear from our ongoing dialogue with teenagers that they use classification in a mature way. While some inevitably seek out 'forbidden fruit', many others use age ratings to avoid content which may disturb them and most use age ratings to protect younger siblings.

We use regular visits to schools and colleges across the UK to survey what young people think about classification. In 2013 we visited over 120 schools, colleges, universities and film festivals, and held seminars and video conferences involving over 11,000 students of all ages. Surveys completed by 841 students visited in schools and colleges at the end of 2012 and beginning of 2013 showed that 81 per cent "totally" or "mainly agreed" with the classifications of films they had seen recently, while 83 per cent of under-eighteens like to find out what's in a film before they see it.

Further research amongst children and young people was carried out in partnership with the Industry Trust for IP Awareness during 2013. The research focused on age-inappropriate viewing and to what extent young people are accessing pirated film content online. The research, which, in July 2013 surveyed 1,000 children aged eleven to fifteen, found that one in five young people (18 per cent) admit they have been disturbed by films they have watched on pirate websites and two thirds (65 per cent) wish they had checked the film's official age rating first. A third (37 per cent) of children aged eleven to twelve admitted to having recently downloaded or streamed a film rated 15 from a pirate website, while more than a quarter of eleven to fifteen year olds (27 per cent) said their parents don't know what films they are watching online, and a third (32 per cent) wouldn't feel comfortable with younger siblings copying their viewing habits.

To help achieve our key goals of protecting children and vulnerable adults and empowering consumers, we provide a number of tools that the public can access easily, some of which they will see each time they visit the cinema or rent or buy a DVD/Blu-ray.

Film classifications and BBFCinsight is included on most film posters, cinema online booking webpages, and age ratings and more detailed BBFCinsight for films can be found on the BBFC website and free BBFC App for iPhone and Android devices. A growing number of online VOD platforms also use BBFC age ratings for films available to stream or download.

Every film shown at the cinema is preceded by a BBFC black card, which shows the age rating, plus the short BBFCinsight for the film, to remind the audience, particularly parents, why the film received a particular classification. For example, the short BBFCinsight shown on the black card for the PG classified film *Frozen*, reads: "Contains mild threat", while the BBFCinsight for the 12A classified James Bond film *Skyfall*, reads: "Contains moderate action violence and one use of strong language". By law, age ratings and short BBFCinsight must also be included on DVD and Blu-ray packaging.

In addition to our regular day-to-day job of protecting children and vulnerable adults from potentially harmful or otherwise unsuitable content through classification, we've also been working with the home entertainment industry, groups concerned with child protection, and the Government, to review whether some material that is exempt from classification under the Video Recordings Act 1984, should lose its exemption from regulation. A recent review into exempt content concluded in 2013 with the Government agreeing to lower the threshold at which content available on DVD/Blu-ray loses its exemption. This means that music, sports, religious and educational content that was previously exempt from classification on video/DVD/Blu-ray, but which contains content unsuitable for children, will require a BBFC classification in future. Such content includes depictions of self-harm, suicide, drug misuse and racist material.

In addition to this, the Government is encouraging us and the UK music industry (represented by the BPI) to devise a voluntary system for classifying music videos available on the internet. We are therefore working in partnership with key record labels and platforms on a pilot for age rating such videos.

A similar pilot is underway in Italy to test an international tool that allows the public to age rate user generated content (UGC), including amateur videos uploaded to video sharing websites. We worked with the Dutch media regulator, NICAM, to develop a prototype tool that consists of a single, easy to use questionnaire which is designed to be completed primarily by people *viewing* the content, though the uploader could also use it to rate his or her own content. The tool gives a different age rating depending on the country you are in when you choose to age rate the content and the result reflects different national sensibilities and societal concerns.

To ensure the public can remain informed about classification decisions, methods and the wider work of the BBFC on initiatives such as the UGC rating tool and the classification framework for mobile network operators, we provide regular BBFC newsletters. The public can subscribe to our monthly public newsletter and our education newsletter, distributed once a term, on our website. Our website for children, www.CBBFC.co.uk provides education focused news, tips and articles for parents and games for younger children. There are further educational resources, including regular podcasts and case studies, for adults and young people interested in, or studying, film classification, on our main website www.bbfc.co.uk. Any member of the public with a query about film classification in general, or feedback about the classification of a film or DVD/Blu-ray they have seen, can contact the BBFC by emailing feedback@bbfc.co.uk. Teachers can also find out about BBFC seminars by visiting our education web page at http://www.bbfc.co.uk/education-resources.

Children's Online and App-based Games 12
Marie Southgate

Parents should have confidence that games promoted for children are compliant with the law.

OFT investigation

In April 2013, the Office of Fair Trading (OFT) announced an investigation into whether children were being unfairly pressured or encouraged to pay for additional content in 'free' web and app-based games, including upgraded membership or virtual currency such as coins, gems or fruit. The OFT had concerns, for example, about games in which players can access only portions of these games for free, with new levels or features – such as faster gameplay – costing money. We launched our investigation to assess whether games were using misleading, aggressive or otherwise unfair commercial practices in breach of consumer protection law.

As part of the investigation, we scrutinised commercial practices in 38 web and app-based games that we considered were likely to appeal to children. The games we examined were produced by businesses in the UK, Europe and the rest of the world.

We also received around 200 submissions in response to our call for information, approximately 160 of which were from parents, the rest mostly from industry stakeholders. We met several industry stakeholders – including individual businesses and trade associations – to discuss our concerns. In July 2013, we hosted a meeting with around 45 industry stakeholders to discuss how compliance in the industry could be improved.

Findings

The OFT published the results of its investigation in September 2013. It found that some games included potentially misleading, aggressive and unfair commercial practices to which children may be particularly susceptible: for example, games implying the player would somehow be letting other players or in-game characters down if they did not obtain something by making an in-game purchase.

The main problems we articulated were:

- A lack of transparent, accurate and clear up-front information relating to, for example, costs, and other information material to a consumer's decision about whether to play, download or sign up to a game

- Misleading commercial practices, including failing to differentiate clearly between commercial messages and gameplay

- Exploitation of children's inexperience, vulnerability and credulity, including by aggressive commercial practices

- The inclusion in games of direct exhortations to children to buy advertised products, or persuade their parents or other adults to buy advertised products for them

- Payments being taken from account holders without their knowledge, express authorisation or informed consent

To address these concerns, the OFT produced a set of draft Principles for online games for consultation in September 2013, which were finalised in January 2014.

We considered that the Principles would be the most helpful and proportionate approach to address the issues we identified during our consultation because they clarify our view of the entire industry's obligations under consumer protection law.

The Principles

The OFT's principles state that:

- Consumers should be told up front about costs associated with a game and about any important information, such as whether the game contains a social networking aspect or whether players' personal data are to be shared with other parties for marketing purposes

- The commercial intent of any in-game promotion of paid-for content, or promotion of any other product or service, should be clear and distinguishable from gameplay

- A game should not mislead consumers by giving the false impression that payments are required or are an integral part of the way the game is played if that is not the case

- Games should not include practices that are aggressive, or which otherwise have the potential to exploit a child's inherent inexperience, vulnerability or credulity or to place undue influence or pressure on a child to make a purchase

- A game should not include direct exhortations to children to make a purchase or persuade others to make purchases for them

- In-game payments are not authorised, and should not be taken, unless the payment account holder, such as a parent, has given his or her express, informed consent

International approach

We shared the Principles with our international consumer enforcement counterparts to ensure that there is as much consistency in regulation as possible, irrespective of where a business is based. We have had discussions on a European level with other Member States through the Consumer Protection Cooperation (CPC) network, and on a broader international level through the International Consumer Protection and Enforcement Network (ICPEN), so that we could develop the Principles to allow them to be applied by other enforcement agencies when interpreting their own domestic consumer protection law. Although there are clearly differences in international consumer protection law outside the EU, there has been significant agreement that the Principles strike a suitable balance and have helped to achieve consistency – as far as possible and where jurisdictional differences permit – in compliance and enforcement strategies.

Since the publication of the finalised Principles, the OFT has participated in EU-wide enforcement discussions. Alongside agencies from other Member States, the OFT met with Apple, Google and an industry representative body, to outline concerns and to set out a common enforcement position, which is consistent with the OFT Principles. These discussions are ongoing and we are optimistic that they will lead to significant improvements.

Advice for parents

The OFT also published guidance for parents to ensure that children are not pressured into making in-game purchases and to reduce the risk of their making unauthorised payments.

Specifically, the OFT advice suggested that parents:

•	Check the 'payment options' settings on their device. One option is to make sure that a password is required for every purchase, rather than opening a 'payment window' in which the password will not be needed for any further payments

•	Check whether there are any in-game purchases or whether the game contains a social element by looking at its description on the app store or the game's website

•	Play the game themselves to understand what children will see

•	Be aware that game content could change via automatic updates, so check regularly that they continue to be happy with their children playing a game

The future

Enforcement of the law underpinning the Principles is obviously important. The Competition and Markets Authority (CMA) took over many of the OFT's responsibilities from 1 April 2014, following the OFT's closure, and picked up from where the OFT left off in respect of children's online games. That includes continuing to contribute to the EU-wide enforcement discussions and monitoring the market to check whether the industry is complying with its legal obligations.

The industry itself is also being encouraged to report non-compliance to the CMA and parents can now get advice from or complain to Citizens Advice about online or app games they have concerns about.

An Overview of Ofcom's Research on Children's Media Literacy

13

Alison Preston

Introduction

The promotion of media literacy is a responsibility placed on Ofcom by Section 11 of the Communications Act 2003. Under Section 14 (6a) of the Act we have a duty to make arrangements for the carrying out of research into the matters mentioned in Section 11 (1).

Ofcom's definition of media literacy is:

"the ability to use, understand and create media and communications in a variety of contexts".

In the online world, it is arguably more important than ever for people to develop these core media literacy skills ("use, understand and create") as well as a range of additional skills specifically related to digital consumption: for example developing the critical evaluation skills to make informed choices about unregulated content, and developing strategies for the management of personal information.

The prism of media literacy is societal or citizen-oriented, adding flesh to the bones of pure consumption and behaviour. Our media literacy research looks at attitudes and motivations and how they all fit together, with an interest in how this impacts upon society in general as well as consumers in particular.

Our *Children and Parents: Media Use and Attitudes Report* is designed to give an accessible overview of media literacy among children and young people aged five to fifteen (and their parents/carers), as well as an overview of media use by children aged three to four. It is an annual report based mainly on survey research conducted in the spring of each year. We have carried out our surveys since 2005 and so can show trends over time across a range of measures.

This article provides an overview of some of the key findings from our 2013 report, which can be found at www.ofcom.org.uk/medialiteracyresearch. Our 2014 report is due for publication in the autumn.

The use of tablets by children aged 5–15 to go online more than doubled between 2012 and 2013

While home use of the internet remained the same since 2011 (84% of children aged five to fifteen), the proportion of children using a mobile phone to go online increased from 22% in 2012 to 27% in 2013. This was driven by an increase among 8-11s and 12-15s saying that they used their phone to go online.

However, the biggest change was in the use of tablets to go online. In 2012, 9% of children said they used a tablet, and, in 2013, 23% said they used one. This increase was evident across all age groups – from 6% to 21% for 5-7s, from 9% to 27% for 8-11s, and from 11% to 22% for 12-15s.

Indeed, in 2013, one in five (19%) online 5-7s used a tablet as their main device to go online, up from 4% in 2012. This contrasts with online 12-15s, of whom one in five (20%) nominate their mobile phone as their main device, and 8% their tablet.

One possible outcome of this development is a more solitary use of the internet. However, our findings don't show any increase in solo online use. 11% of 5-7s, 24% of 8-11s and 52% of 12-15s said they mostly used the internet on their own, with these figures unchanged over the last five years.
The growth of tablets and smartphones are significant shifts in the types of device used, and preferred, by different children for their online activities. To what extent are these shifts part of a more widespread change in children's media habits?

Regular media activities have changed little over time – although reading for 8-15s has decreased since 2012

We have asked the same question since 2007 about whether children do a range of media activities "almost every day". For most activities there has been remarkably little change over time given the changes in digital media devices, although there has been an overall decline in watching DVDs or videos, and listening to the radio. The most significant decrease was in reading magazines, comics or newspapers, with a reduction in the proportion of 8-11s saying they do this: from 41% in 2012 to 31% in 2013; and from 39% of 12-15s in 2012 to 28% in 2013.

FIGURE 1

Devices ever used by children to go online at home, by age: 2011, 2012 and 2013

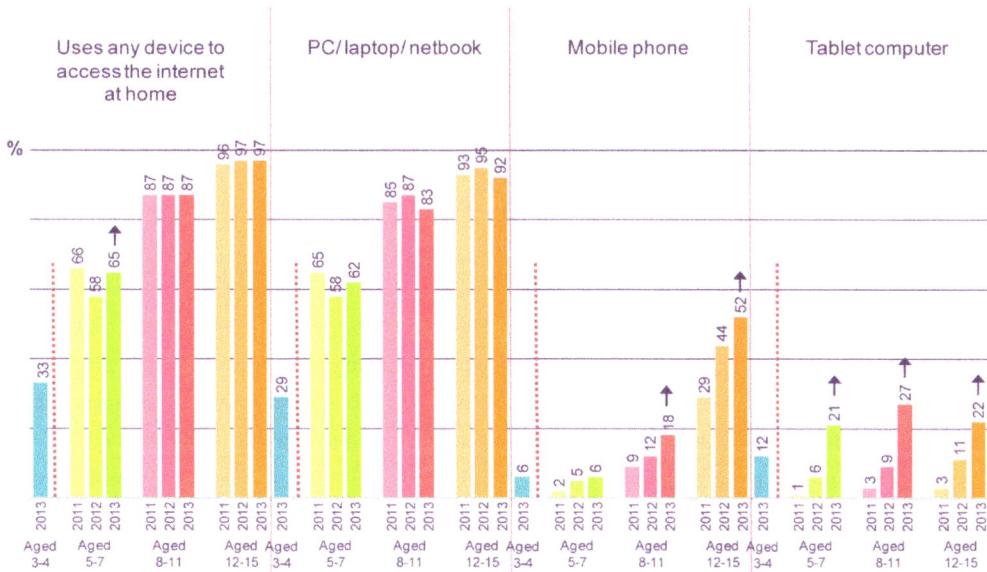

QP3C/ QP26A – I'm going to read out a list of different types of equipment that you may or may not have in your home, and which your child may or may not use / Including any ways you may have already mentioned, does your child ever use any of the following devices to go online at home? (prompted responses, single coded) **RESPONSES SHOWN REFLECT THOSE GIVEN BY 2% OR MORE OF ALL RESPONDENTS IN 2013 – NB The question wording changed at Wave 2 2010 – responses from wave 1 and wave 2 2010 have however been combined. In 2013 responses are taken from the child aged 12-15 rather than the parent, as had been the case in previous years
Base. Parents of children aged 3-4 or 5-15 (685 aged 3-4 in 2013, 573 aged 5-7 in 2011, 570 aged 5-7 in 2012, 533 aged 5-7 in 2013, 586 aged 8-11 in 2011, 575 aged 8-11 in 2012, 587 aged 8-11 in 2013, 558 aged 12-15 in 2011, 572 aged 12-15 in 2012, 569 aged 12-15 in 2013). Significance testing shows any change between 2012 and 2013
Source: Ofcom research, fieldwork carried out by Saville Rossiter-Base in April to June 2013

FIGURE 2

Regular media activities undertaken, by age: 2007, 2009, 2011, 2012 and 2013

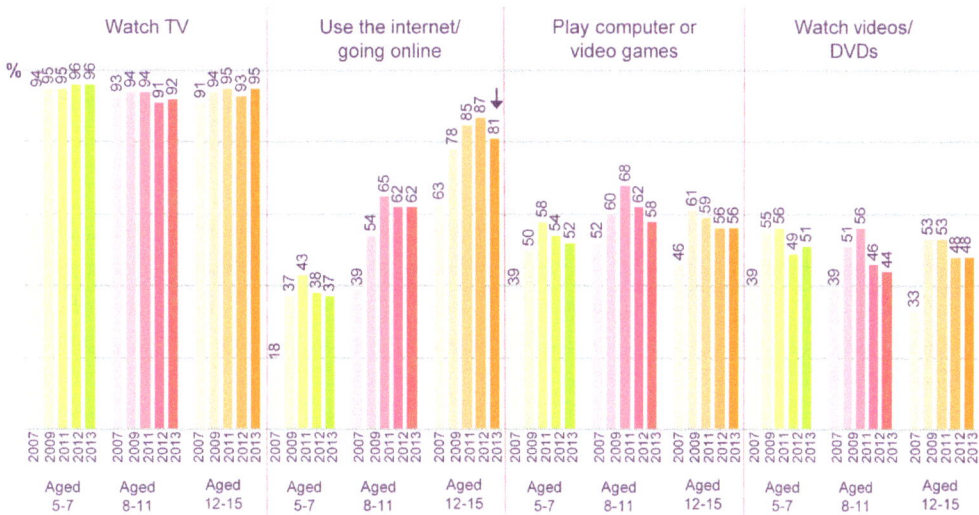

QC52– Which of the following do you do almost every day? (prompted responses, multi-coded)
Base: Children aged 5-15 (985 aged 5-7 in 2007, 576 aged 5-7 in 2009, 573 aged 5-7 in 2011,570 aged 5-7 in 2012, 533 aged 5-7 in 2013, 1354 aged 8-11 in 2007, 774 aged 8-11 in 2009, 586 aged 8-11 in 2011, 575 aged 8-11 in 2012, 587 aged 8-11 in 2013, 1357 aged 12-15 in 2007, 781 aged 12-15 in 2009, 558 aged 12-15 in 2011, 572 aged 12-15 in 2012, 569 aged 12-15 in 2013). Significance testing shows any differences between 2012 and 2013
Source: Ofcom research, fieldwork carried out by Saville Rossiter-Base in April to June 2013

TV programmes are being watched on different devices

For all age groups, watching TV remains important. For 5-7s and 8-11s, time spent watching TV is significantly greater than using other forms of media. For 12-15s, it is at similar levels to using the internet. When asked which type of activity they would miss the most, nearly six in ten 5-7s nominated TV (57%), and four in ten 8-11s (42%). However, only one in five 12-15s (19%) did so, and they were twice as likely to nominate using a mobile phone (39%).

The resonance of television is somewhat masked by the increasing convergence of available platforms to watch TV content. As Figure 3 shows, in 2013 children were increasingly likely to watch TV programmes on devices other than their TV set, with over four in ten 5-15s using alternative devices to watch TV content. This was a significant increase since 2012 (45% vs 34%) and reflects the growth in tablets, with 15% of 5-15s watching TV programmes on tablets. While 14% of 5-15s said they used a mobile phone to watch TV programmes, this rose to 25% of 12-15s.

Most online activities vary by age group, with the exception of playing games

Figure 4 sets out what children are doing online on a weekly or more frequent basis. Playing games was the most popular activity in 2013 for 3-4s and 5-7s, while homework was the most common activity for 8-11s and 12-15s. Compared to 2012, older children were less likely to visit social media sites and more likely to use IM (instant messaging). For older children, communication is the core activity, while for younger children narrative-based content is more compelling.

Fewer children say they have social networking profiles, but there is an increase in the variety of sites being used

A key form of communication, particularly for older age groups, is, of course, social networking. However, it is of note that compared to 2012, 12-15s were less likely in 2013 to say they had set up a social networking site profile (68% vs 81%). There was also a decrease since 2012 in the number of children aged between 8-12 (underage users) with an active profile on Facebook, Bebo or MySpace (22%, down from 30% in 2012).

FIGURE 3

Devices ever used by children aged 5-15 to watch television programmes at home: 2012 and 2013

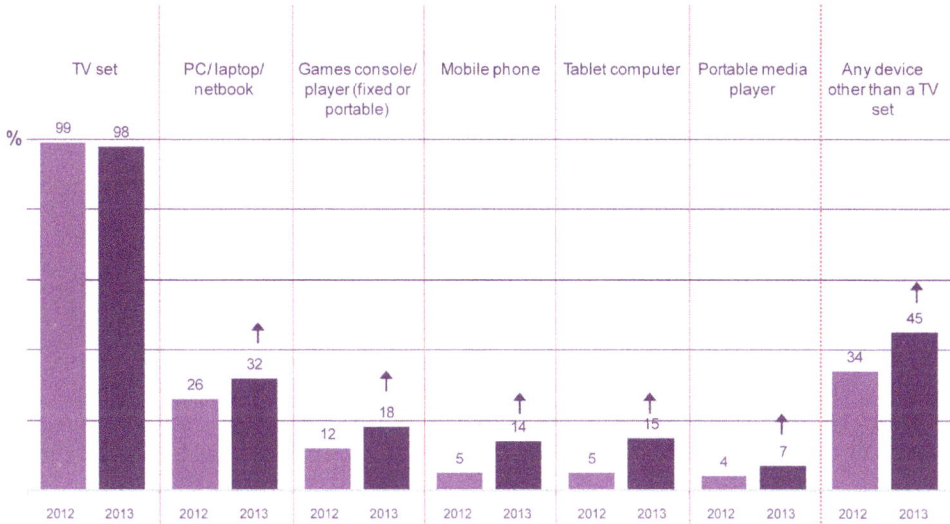

TV set	PC/laptop/ netbook	Games console/ player (fixed or portable)	Mobile phone	Tablet computer	Portable media player	Any device other than a TV set
99 / 98	26 / 32	12 / 18	5 / 14	5 / 15	4 / 7	34 / 45
2012 / 2013	2012 / 2013	2012 / 2013	2012 / 2013	2012 / 2013	2012 / 2013	2012 / 2013

QP5 – Does your child EVER use any of these devices to watch television programmes at home? (prompted responses, multi-coded)
Base: Parents of children aged 3-4 or 5-15 (685 aged 3-4 in 2013, 1717 aged 5-15 in 2012, 1689 aged 5-15 in 2013). In 2013 responses are taken from the child aged 12-15 rather than the parent, as had been the case in previous years
Significance testing shows any change between 2012 and 2013
Source: Ofcom research, fieldwork carried out by Saville Rossiter-Base in April to June 2013

FIGURE 4

Top ten internet activities carried out at least once a week, by age: 2013

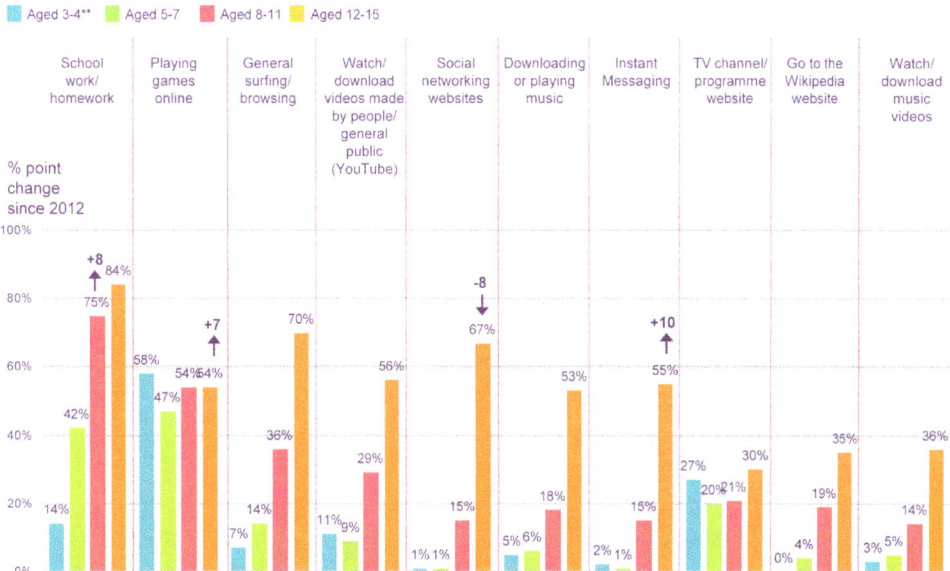

Legend: Aged 3-4** | Aged 5-7 | Aged 8-11 | Aged 12-15

QC14A-U– When you're at home, do you go online to do any of these things? Please think about going online on any type of computer, mobile phone, games player or media player (prompted responses, single coded) – PERCENTAGES SHOWN REFLECT THOSE THAT UNDERTAKE ACTIVITY AT LEAST WEEKLY **QUESTION ASKED OF PARENTS FOR 3-4S AND CHILDREN AGED 5-15
Base: Parents of 3-4s and children aged 5-15 who use the internet at home (219 parents of 3-4s, 1424 aged 5-15 in 2012, 1426 aged 5-7 in 2012, 376 aged 5-7 in 2012, 381 aged 5-7 in 2013, 495 aged 8-11 in 2012, 497 aged 8-11 in 2013, 553 aged 12-15 in 2012, 548 aged 12-15 in 2013). Significance testing shows any change between 2012 and 2013.
Source: Ofcom research, fieldwork carried out by Saville Rossiter-Base in April to June 2013

FIGURE 5

Proportion of children who use the internet at home with an active social networking site profile, by individual age: 2013

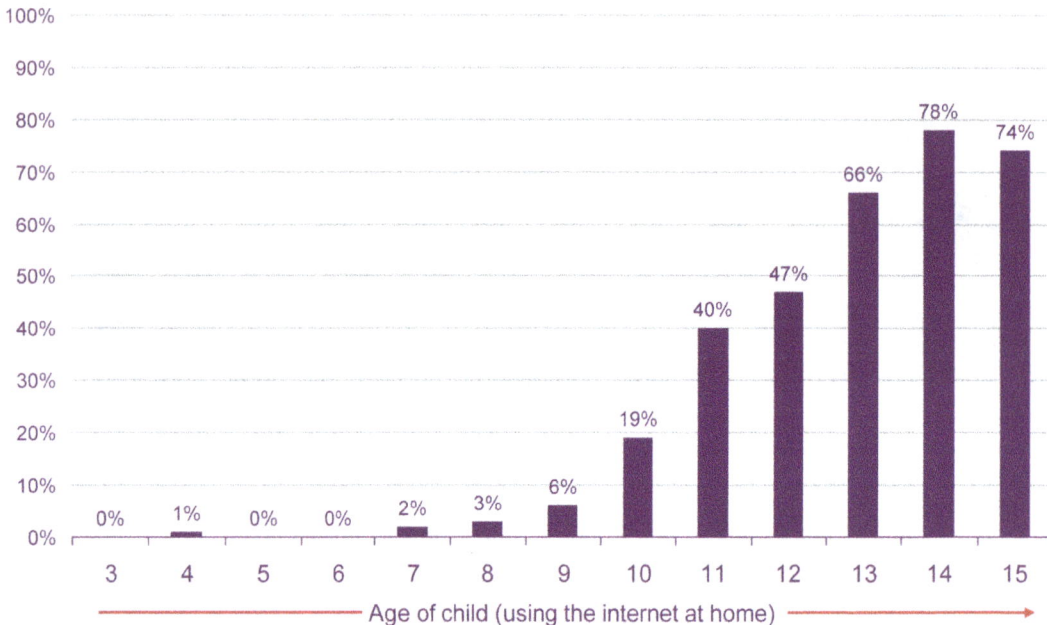

QC21A – Which different social networking sites do you have a page or profile on? (spontaneous responses, multicoded)
Base: Parent of children aged 3-7 and children aged 8-15 who use the internet at at home (101 aged 3, 118 aged 4, 145 aged 5, 103 aged 6, 133 aged 7, 143 aged 8, 116 aged 9, 132 aged 10, 106 aged 11, 180 aged 12, 99 aged 13, 110 aged 14, 159 aged 15)
Source: Ofcom research, fieldwork carried out by Saville Rossiter-Base in April to June 2013

While nearly all 12-15s (97%) with a social networking profile said they had a Facebook profile, there was an increase in 12-15s with a profile on Twitter: 37% of social networkers had a profile compared to 25% in 2012. Boys were more likely than girls to have a profile on YouTube (31% vs 21%) while girls were more likely to have a profile on Tumblr (12% vs 4%). One in six (16%) said they had a profile on Instagram.

This age group were most likely to use their smartphone to visit their social networking sites: 41% of 12-15s with an active profile said they used their mobile phone as their main device to access their social networking (34% said they used a laptop/netbook as their main device, 13% a PC and 7% a tablet).

While social media of course remains a dominant activity for most (older) children, it is possible to see the beginnings of a shift in focus towards more short-term, brief, 'disposable' types of communication such as Twitter, IM and Instagram.

Children's critical awareness is variable

This final section sets out some of the responses to the questions we ask children to gauge the extent of their critical awareness.

As background context, it's useful to remind ourselves of the extent to which children are navigating widely across the web, and thereby encountering new content. When asked whether, in most weeks, they tended to visit new sites or not, six in ten (61%) of 8-11s agreed that they "only visit websites they have visited before", and three in ten (31%) agreed they "visit maybe one or two websites they haven't visited before". Only 3% agreed that they "visit lots of websites they haven't visited before". 12-15s were marginally more likely to navigate more widely, with 9% saying they visit lots of new sites, but still just under half (49%) said they only visited websites they'd been to previously. There was little change since 2011, although 8-11s were slightly more likely to visit one or two new websites during this period.

Despite this relatively limited navigation, it is important that children have some kind of critical understanding of the desirability of making some kinds of checks when visiting a new website. What types of checks do they tend to make? Two-thirds (66%) of online 12-15s said they made any kind of check when visiting a new site, a similar proportion since 2011. They were most likely to nominate checking the general appearance of the site (28%) and how up to date it was (26%). There was however a decrease since 2012 in making checks to see if there was a padlock or other type of symbol to indicate the site was secure – from 26% in 2012 to 20% in 2013. Conversely, more 12-15s used the site being up to date as a check in 2013 than they did in 2012 (26% vs 18% in 2012).

Turning to search engine navigation, which is as ubiquitous for older children as it is for adults, it is useful to gauge the extent to which children trust the results that are provided by the search engine, and whether they think about the provenance of the content.

When asked about the results listed by search engines, 45% of 12-15s who used search engines agreed that some of the information in the list will be accurate and some won't be. However, one third (32%) thought that if the results have come from the search engine then they must be truthful, while 15% didn't think about such matters and simply used the sites they like the look of. Over time, these figures have changed little.

In summary, children's media habits have changed considerably in the last couple of years in terms of the devices used to go online. There has been a rapid growth in tablets across all age groups, and smartphones for older children are now embedded in their daily lives. The use of social media continues to develop, with older children seeming to move towards more disposable, short-term messaging applications. However, attitudes to various aspects of being online appear to have changed little, and TV and games remain popular activities for most children.

What Does Good Content Look Like? Developing Great Online Content for Kids

14

Sonia Livingstone

The challenge

> The child/media relationship is an entry point into the wide and multifaceted world of children and their rights – to education, freedom of expression, play, identity, health, dignity and self-respect, protection … in every aspect of child rights, in every element of the life of a child, the relationship between children and the media plays a role.[1]

Think back twenty years to society's early hopes for mass internet access – the prospect of a world of information at your fingertips, making friends across the globe, working and learning anywhere anytime, digital opportunity overcoming socio-economic disadvantage. Ten years later, the advent of web 2.0 added more hopes – everyone able to create content and participate in online communities, exploring and tailoring their online lives to enhance life offline. Distinctively, children – among the world's poorest, the last to benefit from technological developments – were the pioneers in this exciting digital world and, for once, adults learned from them.

How, then, shall we view the top ten sites visited by UK six to fourteen year olds in 2013: 63 per cent visited Google, 40 per cent YouTube, 34 per cent BBC, 27 per cent Facebook, 21 per cent Yahoo, seventeen per cent Disney, seventeen per cent Wikipedia, sixteen per cent Amazon, sixteen per cent MSC and fifteen per cent eBay.[2] To be sure, the list includes a 'long tail' of esoteric sites meeting specific interests, but if you talk to children about their browsing patterns, they say that Google, YouTube, Facebook, CBBC and a handful of other sites capture most, if not all, of what they do online. And they look a little blank if you ask about the kinds of sites that excite the attention of the internet geeks and entrepreneurs. Indeed, 55 per cent of eight to fifteen year old internet users say that mostly they only visit websites they have visited before. And although most have made a social network profile, few have participated in more creative or civic activities. In short, most children don't get far up the 'ladder of online opportunities'.[3]

Is it what children themselves really want? Or what we want for them? Who are 'we' to judge what's good for children? These are difficult questions. My interest is in normative rather than descriptive judgements – in distinguishing what is positively beneficial for children's wellbeing from observations of what children actually like or choose to do. I would love there to be more and better opportunities for children online, and I would also love them to know more about the fabulous opportunities that do exist but which most haven't heard of.

Since we do not live in a perfect world, I assume more can be done to design an online environment that advances children's needs and interests. And although children are not the sole arbiter of what is good for them, I am motivated by knowing that they are only partially satisfied with the online offer.[4] I also assume that many organisations would like to provide great content for children and young people but may be uncertain how to conceive of it or to design it. Therefore I hope to stimulate public and professional debate over 'what good looks like.'

What do children need?

How can we set positive goals for children without sounding pious or elitist? Increasingly, policy makers and child welfare advocates use the concept of 'wellbeing' to articulate an open-minded, ambitious yet practical approach, based on evidence of what advantages or disadvantages children's life chances.[5] To paraphrase the 2013 *Good Childhood Report*, children and young people need:

- The right conditions to learn and develop
- A positive view of themselves and a respect for their identity
- Enough of the items and experiences that matter to them
- Positive relationships with their family, friends and school
- A safe and suitable home environment and local area
- The opportunities to take part in positive activities that help them thrive

This surely pinpoints the main purpose of provision to meet children's needs online as well as offline. It may be thought that such considerations justify dedicated resources for young children, but that teenagers are already sufficiently media-savvy, able to meet their own needs from the resources of the adult world. Without undermining efforts to extend online opportunities for ever younger children, I suggest that this should not lead to the neglect of teenagers, for their very different needs are also significant as they struggle to find autonomy, identity and support in an uncertain world. Famously, they are a demanding group, difficult for parents to support and critical in their response to much of what is designed for them. But efforts can and should be made, because of the problems that beset them and because the UNCRC defines 'the child', for the purposes of ensuring provision, protection and participation rights, as all those under eighteen years old.

To apply such purposes to the internet, we need some more specific guiding principles. A few years ago, I adapted the principles laid down in the internationally-endorsed though rarely enacted Children's Television Charter[6] to propose a Children's Internet Charter[7] which asserts the importance of quality, affirmation, diversity, protection, inclusion, cultural heritage and support. Again I paraphrase:

1. Children should have online contents and services of high **quality** which are made specifically for them, and which do not take advantage of them or exploit them. In addition to entertaining, these should allow children to develop physically, mentally and socially to their fullest potential

2. Children should be able to hear, see and express themselves, their culture, their languages and their life experiences, through online contents and services which **affirm** their sense of self, community and place

3. Children's online contents and services should promote an awareness and appreciation of **diverse** other cultures in parallel with the child's own cultural background

4. Children's online contents and services should be wide-ranging in genre and content, but should **protect** them from exposure to gratuitous violence or pornography inappropriate to their age or maturity

5. Children's online contents and services should be **inclusive** and accessible to all, building on knowledge of when and where children are available to engage, and capitalising on widely accessible media or technologies

6. Governments, production, distribution and funding organisations should recognise and protect the importance of children's indigenous cultural and linguistic **heritage** through provision of sufficient online contents and services

7. Funds must be made available to **support** the production and availability of these online contents and services to the highest possible standards

These principles are not as straightforward in practice as they may seem stated in the abstract. Questions of standards, quality and diversity are particularly difficult. For instance, supporting children and young people as they develop their identities, especially their sexuality, gives rise to lively cultural contestation regarding the appropriate forms of information and guidance. Then, many sites are very 'sticky', keeping users on the site rather than encouraging children to explore. There are two main reasons for this. One concerns the promotion of the brand such that indicators of effectiveness prioritise time spent on the site: this is certainly true for commercial sites but even for many public and third sector sites. The other concerns safety: since it is expensive if not impossible to guarantee that links to other sites will not lead a child user towards risk, the most risk-averse strategy is to avoid any links. But the resulting walled gardens risk closing down children's opportunities rather than structuring positive pathways of exploration across multiple sites and resources.

Furthermore, one must acknowledge that demanding dedicated, age-appropriate content poses severe funding challenges, especially in smaller language communities and especially if a commercial underpinning is to be restricted or eliminated. Lastly, children and – especially – teenagers, have a positive desire to find contents that are precisely disapproved of by adults: many games sites fall into this category, especially multiplayer online worlds. Among researchers the jury is still out regarding the benefits, partly because much depends on the content, the child and how the content is used by children in particular contexts.

Practical suggestions

As jury chair of the European Commission's Award for Best Content for Kids, I and an expert group of content producers, child welfare experts and youth representatives reviewed the 67 shortlisted entries, selected from 1,130 submissions in 26 countries, to choose the European winners in four content categories – those created by adult non-professionals, adult professionals, individual young people (under eighteen years old) and school/youth groups.[8] There was much to applaud among the submissions but also room for improvement. To guide our judgements, we focused on three broad criteria: anticipated benefit, attractiveness and usability, drawing on the European POSCON project for its practical thinking about creating online content to benefit children.[9]

Rather than restating these as normative demands on content developers, I will conclude by formulating some key questions to bear in mind when planning, producing and evaluating content. While the principle of support applies to all, these questions operationalise the earlier-mentioned principles, recognising that the overall purpose will only be achieved if content provision is clear-sighted in its anticipated benefits, attractive to children and readily usable by them.

Anticipated benefit (cf. the principles of quality, affirmation and protection)

- Does the content aim to stimulate and support children's imagination, understanding or self-expression?[10]
- Does the content enable children to recognise themselves as agents in the world, even opening up pathways for action?
- Is the content designed to be age-appropriate, including supporting resources for parents or teachers?
- Have potentially harmful features been identified and either eliminated or effectively addressed?[11]

Attractiveness (cf. the principles of diversity and cultural heritage)

• Does the content meet high production standards and is it appealing to children – creative, enriching and without boring or stereotyped features?
• Is the content genuinely informed by children's own voices, respecting and reflecting their diverse experiences and life contexts, rather than imposing adult expectations or norms upon them?[12]

Usability (cf. the principle of inclusion)

• Is the navigation structure user-friendly, so that young and novice users neither get lost within the site nor find themselves unexpectedly outside it?
• Is the content usable on multiple devices – especially those used by children – and in languages appropriate to the anticipated user group?
• Is the design of available resources transparent in terms of production, aims and funding?

As I noted at the outset, we are still at an early stage in designing the internet we want for children – certainly by comparison with the longer history of books, film, music, television or games. In relation to more established media, there are high profile competitions, celebrity advocates and high status rewards for producing and distributing great content for children. In the UK, the most prominent are probably the BAFTA awards – which include children's feature films, animation, learning resources, video games and, now, websites and other digital/interactive contents. Internationally, the Prix Jeunesse Foundation celebrates the best in children's television, and there are many prizes for the best children's books.

But we need more for the internet, both to promote what is being achieved and to build capacity in this new domain. My hope is that we will not be complacent about the quantity of online content available for children while forgetting to ask about its quality. That children spontaneously spend many hours online does not necessarily mean that all is well. Rather, I hope we can open up debate over the criteria and expectations by which society can provide for children's communication needs and rights in the digital age. Let's see what good we can do, if we really put our minds to it.

Endnotes

1 UNICEF's Oslo Challenge. This was issued on the tenth anniversary of the United Nations' Convention on the Rights of the Child (1989). It challenged nations to recognise the role of media and communications in advancing children's rights in the digital age: http://www.unicef.org/magic/briefing/oslo.html.

2 Adapted from COMSCORE data in the annex to Ofcom (2013). *Children and parents: Media use and attitudes report*. London: Office of Communications. Available at http://stakeholders.ofcom.org.uk/binaries/research/media-literacy/october-2013/research07Oct2013.pdf

3 See Livingstone and Helsper (2007) on gradations in youthful digital inclusion at http://eprints.lse.ac.uk/2768/ This shows the low engagement of most children and young people and the fact that those who engage more are often more privileged in socio-economic terms. These findings were updated in Livingstone, et al (2011) EU Kids Online II: Final Report, at http://eprints.lse.ac.uk/39351/

4 In 2010, four in ten UK 9-16 year olds said it is only 'a bit true' that there are lots of good things for them to do online. See the UK findings from the pan-European survey conducted by the EU Kids Online network at http://eprints.lse.ac.uk/33730/ Further, there was no improvement in a 2013 update of this survey. See Mascheroni, G. & Ólafsson, K. (2014). *Net Children Go Mobile: risks and opportunities*. Milano: Educatt. Available at http://www.netchildrengomobile.eu/

5 For example,
https://www.gov.uk/government/uploads/system/uploads/attachment_data/file/183197/Child-Wellbeing-Brief.pdf and
http://www.unicef.org.uk/UNICEFs-Work/What-we-do/Issues-we-work-on/Child-well-being/
For a review of the evidence relevant to the media, see
http://webarchive.nationalarchives.gov.uk/20130401151715_
https://www.education.gov.uk/publications/eOrderingDownload/00669-2009DOM-EN.pdf

6 The Children's Television Charter, proposed by Anna Home in 1995, is here: http://www.wsmcf.com/charters/charter.htm

7 A children's internet charter, drawing on the UN Convention on the Rights of the Child and articulating a rationale for positive online content for children, is here: http://eprints.lse.ac.uk/48922/

8 See http://www.bestcontentaward.eu/home

9 See their work and guidance here: http://www.positivecontent.eu/about-poscon-1/

10 In their UNICEF guidance on communicating with children, Barbara Kolucki and Dafna Lemish articulate "principles and practices to nurture, inspire, excite, educate and heal": http://www.unicef.org/cbsc/files/CwC_Web(2).pdf

11 BBC guidelines on youth contributors are helpful here: http://www.bbc.co.uk/editorialguidelines/page/guidelines-children-introduction/ So too are UKKCIS' moderation guidelines: https://www.gov.uk/government/uploads/system/uploads/attachment_data/file/251457/industry_guidance_moderation.pdf. For e-safety, see the Safer Internet Centre: http://www.saferinternet.org.uk/advice-and-resources. On advertising to children online, see guidance from the ASA: http://www.asa.org.uk/News-resources/Hot-Topics/Children-and-advertising.aspx and the OFT: http://www.oft.gov.uk/shared_oft/consumer-enforcement/oft1519.pdf

12 In a recent study, I contrasted producers' and teenagers' interpretations of websites to show how the former fail to anticipate the latter: http://eprints.lse.ac.uk/2769/

Does Using Tablets in School Make Children Safer Online? 15

Barbie Clarke

Background

An increasing number of children are using mobile devices,[1] especially tablets, and some are able to use tablets in schools as part of their learning. While many can see the benefit of children having their own internet-enabled device in school, there can be concern that this will expose them to content and behaviour that will make them unsafe. Parents especially can be concerned about this. It is a subject that Tablets for Schools has explored.

Tablets for Schools is a UK charity set up by a group of companies in the technology and education world including Carphone Warehouse, Dixons, Google, Samsung, Talk Talk, Virgin Media, Pearson, Microsoft and 9ine.[2] Its aim is to allow every child in school to have their own tablet device, with three overall objectives:

- The democratisation of education
- The personalisation of education for pupils
- Teaching pupils the skills they need for the 21st century

The notion of every child in a school having their own internet-enabled device is becoming a reality in many schools. When we at Family Kids and Youth were first approached by Tablets for Schools to carry out research in 2012, there were only five schools in the UK that had adopted one-to-one tablet devices. Now we have 40 schools in our research programme.

Online safety and cyber-security is a subject that schools are tackling as it becomes clear that children are more technologically-savvy than many adults and yet may lack the skills to keep themselves safe. It has recently been announced by the Department for Business, Innovation and Skills that children aged eleven to fourteen will receive cyber-security lessons, and teachers will be receiving training to prepare them to teach these skills to their pupils.[3]

Family Kids and Youth asked over 3,500 eleven to seventeen year olds in tablet-using schools about online safety[4] to coincide with Safer Internet Day on February 11.[5]

Net savvy kids

The good news is that pupils who are using one-to-one tablets in school are very internet literate, and are taking steps to protect their privacy. The research found that eight out of ten (82 per cent) young people claim to know how to change their privacy settings on social networks such as Facebook or Twitter, or websites such as Google and YouTube, to restrict what other people can see on their profile.

Other steps to protect privacy include three quarters (74 per cent) who only accept friend requests from people they know. Six out of ten (62 per cent) are careful not to post personal information online, and two-thirds (66 per cent) agree with the statement, "I think very carefully about what people might say about me before I post pictures or comments online." Seven out of ten (71 per cent) pupils in tablet-using schools believe that most people their age are aware of how to use the internet safely.

Age makes a difference. Thirteen to sixteen year olds are particularly aware of this with nearly nine out of ten (88 per cent) saying they would be cautious about posting pictures or comments online, although this dropped to seven out of ten (70 per cent) amongst eleven to thirteen year olds, and six out of ten (60 per cent) of pupils in sixth form.

> Remember, if you give out personal info or pictures it's like putting a billboard outside your house of all your personal info and leaving your front door wide open. Think before you do anything online. *Year 7 Girl*

> Don't put anything on the internet you would not want your parents to see. Some employers look at your personal information on the internet to see if you are sensible. *Year 9 Girl*

> My advice is to treat the internet like what it truly is, an area where everyone can speak to anyone, there will be nice people and people who will want to hurt others, so if you treat it like what it is and don't do things you wouldn't normally do then you will be safe. *Year 10 Boy*

> Be sensible. Anyone and everyone can see what you're posting. Just think, would you really want your mum, your teachers, your cousins to see you swearing and being so rude like that at a fellow student over Facebook? Or that compromising photo you sent to your boyfriend who promised he wouldn't show anyone – what happens if you break up? He's got that picture forever and anyone can see it. Think before you act. *Year 10 Girl*

Tablet-using pupils are also very astute about the credibility of what others post online. Half (50 per cent) do not think that people are honest when they post things on websites such as Facebook, Twitter or Instagram.

Talking to Pupils about Safer Internet Use

Having an internet-enabled device that is used in school appears to prompt discussion about safety and security. Parents and teachers in those schools where each pupil is using their own tablet computer are actively talking to young people about being safe online. Nine out of ten (89 per cent) pupils say that their school is doing this, and nearly seven out of ten (67 per cent) pupils report that their parents are talking to them about being safe online. This is particularly high among eleven to thirteen year olds (years 7 and 8) with eight out of ten (80 per cent) saying their parents talk to them about being safe online, although still highly prevalent in the older age groups with six out of ten (60 per cent) thirteen to sixteen year olds (years 9-11) and, interestingly, nearly half (45 per cent) of sixth form pupils having parental discussions about online safety.

Parents and schools are most commonly talking to pupils about not giving out personal information. Virtually all (95 per cent) pupils who use tablets in school report that their school warns them about giving out personal information, and nine out of ten (90 per cent) report that their parents do this. Schools and parents speaking to pupils about not talking online to people they do not know is also common (90 per cent schools, 84 per cent parents). Over three quarters (77 per cent) of pupils report that their school talks to them about how to treat others online.

> If you are worried or concerned tell your parents, carers, teachers, even friends. Telling someone you know makes such a difference, a weight and a half will be lifted off your shoulders. *Year 7 Girl*

> It is not wrong to use the internet or go on social networks but be careful on what you go on. Make sure you don't talk to strangers and keep your account on private at all times. Make sure you report someone or something that is hurting you online. Try talking to teachers, your friends or someone who you trust about something that is worrying you. They will try and look for a solution. *Year 11 Girl*

Schools and parents impose restrictions. But blocking access to websites or apps is much more prevalent at school than at home. Over eight out of ten (85 per cent) pupils report that their school blocks access to certain websites or devices; and thirteen per cent are unsure whether this is the case. When asked however about their school blocking wi-fi access to specific games such as *Call of Duty* or *Grand Theft Auto*, and social networking sites such as Twitter or Snapchat virtually all (96 per cent) say these are blocked.

Parental blocks or restrictions to websites or content appear not to be so strict at home. Nearly one in five pupils says their parents or carers block access to websites at home (seventeen per cent). Over half (56 per cent) believe their parents or carers do not impose restrictions, although over a quarter (28 per cent) are unsure.

Still more work to be done

Despite being internet-savvy, and talking to teachers and parents about staying safe online, over a half (55 per cent) of young people in tablet-using schools agree that, "Many children go on websites they know they should not go on." And over a quarter (27 per cent) have seen something that has concerned, upset or frightened them online.

Despite their best efforts, parents may not be aware of this because when a child had seen something that concerned, upset or frightened them online, over half (54 per cent) dealt with this by telling their friends, and while over one-third (36 per cent) told their parents, a quarter (25 per cent) did not tell anyone about their experience.

And it is hard for a parent to monitor. Nearly two-thirds (64 per cent) of young people interviewed are taking an internet enabled device to bed with them at night. The likelihood of this increases with age, with less than half (48 per cent) of eleven to thirteen year olds (Year 7-8) doing this, rising to nearly three quarters (72 per cent) of thirteen to sixteen year olds (Years 9-11) and nearly nine out of ten (87 per cent) in the sixth form.

Pupils are mostly using their device in bed to look at YouTube or other film or picture websites (64 per cent) and to talk to their friends (66 per cent). But nearly a third are using it to read (32 per cent) and, perhaps worryingly, to do their homework (31 per cent).

> Not everyone and everything is who/what they seem on the internet. Treat people online with the respect you would give people face to face; just because you're behind a keyboard doesn't mean you cannot get into trouble. *Year 8 Boy*

> The internet is like the world. It can be horrible, it can be amazing but you choose which way or path you take. *Year 8 Boy*

Building resilience – working out how to be safe online is preparing them for the future

So while adolescents using tablets in school appear to be well clued up on security and safety, there is undoubtedly some risky behaviour going on. Schools take this very seriously, and many of our tablet schools hold regular parents' evenings, have 'Safer Internet Weeks' once a term, and circulate newsletters and blogs about online safety. It seems that having a one-to-one tablet device opens up a dialogue which can be used to highlight issues such as bullying, cyber-security and issues of trust and authenticity. But adolescents are not risk averse, and they are likely to explore and experiment online in the way that adolescents always have in the offline world. What is clear is that as well as engaging in dialogue about security and safety with parents and teachers, they are also sharing their experiences with friends. Much of the activity that goes on in their private world, when they use their device away from parental or teacher supervision, is likely to be typical of any adolescent behaviour.

One of the drivers behind the charity Tablets for Schools is a recognition that the digital world will be an integral part of these adolescents' future, both in their continuing education and training and their future jobs and careers. To become familiar with the risks and challenges, as well as the opportunities and benefits that such digital devices offer while still young gives them a head start. Much of the learning that is occurring through using their own tablet at school is self-led. They are encouraged to find things out for themselves and to make judgements about the quality of content they view. There are new models of learning developing, such as 'flipped learning' where the teaching happens at home through webinars, MOOCs (Massively Open Online Courses) and video lectures; what used to be homework is now done in class with teachers offering more personalised guidance and interaction with pupils, instead of lecturing.

Learning to be safe, taking risks, making judgements is an integral part of the new world of learning and teaching as well as an important process of adolescence. Using a tablet for education, communication and entertainment enables young people to build a level of resilience that they may not have had before.

Endnotes

1 Ofcom, 2013. Children and Parents: Media Use and Attitudes Report. http://stakeholders.ofcom.org.uk/binaries/research/media-literacy/october-2013/research07Oct2013.pdf

2 Tablets for Schools. http://www.tabletsforschools.org.uk/

3 Cyber Security Skills (2014) BIS.
https://www.gov.uk/government/news/school-children-as-young-as-11-to-get-cyber-security-lessons

4 This survey was sent to nine secondary schools which have been using one-to-one tablets for over a year and are taking part in the Tablets for Schools research programme. The survey was completed online between 13 and 22 January 2014. In total over 3,500 responses were received (total 3,542) from pupils aged eleven to eighteen (49 per cent girls and 51 per cent boys). Two per cent of the sample were aged eighteen, and for the purposes of analysis have been removed from the sample. One school was in Scotland, the remaining eight schools were spread across England, from Northumberland in the north-east, to Cornwall in the south-west, Essex and Kent in the south-east and Bath in the west. Based on a fully completed sample size (all questions responded to) at the 99 per cent confidence level the confidence interval is +/- 2.19.

5 Safer Internet Day, 2014 http://www.saferinternet.org.uk/safer-internet-day/2014/

The Point of News
Young People, Critical Literacy and Citizenship

16

Cynthia Carter

On 29 January 2014, philosopher and author Alain de Botton's five minute film, in which he asks what is the point of news in society, was aired on BBC Two's flagship news and current affairs programme, *Newsnight*. What is perhaps most intriguing to those of us who research and produce factual media for children is that de Botton begins the film with the suggestion that schools ought to teach children how to critically analyse the news (Vale 2014). Schools get it wrong, he suggests, because:

> they teach you how to analyse books and pictures, but no one tells you how to make sense of that far more powerful, questionable art form, the news. We are taught to decode Shakespeare, but not the celebrity section of the Daily Mail, George Elliot but not The Sun, and yet the news is the most powerful force out there shaping how we view political and economic reality. No wonder revolutionaries head to the TV or radio stations first whenever they want to change stuff.

Whilst these points seem largely reasonable, on the following day, de Botton's intervention provoked impassioned debate amongst academics contributing to the Media, Communication and Cultural Studies Association (MeCCSA) discussion list.[1] One senior academic kicked off the exchange alerting colleagues to the film and the ensuing ten minute *Newsnight* studio chat that included de Botton, journalist Samira Ahmed and former Director for Communications, Alistair Campbell. Of de Botton, one academic declared, "He appeared to [be] unaware of the existence of Media Studies. None of the panel [...] challenged his ill informed views." A further contributor contended that, "the *Newsnight* researchers were either too ignorant or too snobbish to invite any of the many distinguished media theorists who might have contributed to the panel – and who are now contributing to the thread." On a different point, another academic concluded: "It's also quite funny that they were unaware of the annual BBC Schools News project which is aimed at thirteen year olds. They believe it ticks the box for 'kids studying news' – I think they're mistaken and said so in the BFI/Ofcom research report *Lifeblood of Democracy? Learning about broadcast news* (see Bazalgette, Harkand and James 2008)."

Attention then turned to teaching children how to critique the news, which all agreed should be a central concern for democratic society, not just media academics. Wide-ranging opinions were voiced, with some pointing out that Media Studies has long been offered at A-level (although very often depicted in the news media as a 'Mickey Mouse' subject) and more recently as a GCSE. Thus, de Botton appeared to be unaware of longstanding efforts that schools have already made to support children's news literacy. That said, others suggested that de Botton was correct if he was referring to the curriculum for young children. As one contributor commented, "The issue here is 5-14 curriculum! You think those kids don't watch the news?"

And of course they do. Most children know what is happening in the news, whether they gain their information from television, radio, newspapers, online, or from what their parents, siblings, schoolmates and teachers have said.

Certainly, there are a number of pressing issues to be addressed around the development of children's news literacy and citizenship. Here I only have the space to explore three that emerge from my experiences researching in the field of children and news. These constitute challenges that would be productively tackled, in my view, through strategic alliances between news producers, media regulators, schools, academics and young people. What form they might take is an open question. My hope is that what I'm outlining here might help to spark interest and engagement in cross-domain research partnerships aiming to better understand – with a view to enhancing – young citizens' engagement with the news.

Issue 1
Critical news literacy
Case study: Hillhead Primary School, Glasgow

Shortly after the attacks on the US on September 11, 2001, one of the producers of the Channel 4 weekly schools news programme, *First Edition*, offered a colleague access to letters written to producers by a class of Year 7 pupils at Hillhead Primary School in Glasgow. In these letters, children provided their reactions to the events of 9/11, demonstrating a critical awareness of how both adult news and *First Edition* had covered the story. Ordinarily each week this group of pupils and their teacher used one English lesson to view and discuss *First Edition*. Children then wrote to producers to comment on the choice of stories, presentation, and their thoughts about the events covered. The teacher, who developed this idea to help her students improve their verbal and written skills, believed this approach would also give the children an opportunity to learn something about the world and about how journalists cover it. After reading through a one year sample of the children's letters, a small group of us developed a research project to explore children's responses to traumatic news events.[2]

In June 2002, we travelled to Glasgow to speak to the pupils who had written the letters to *First Edition*. What we found was that these eleven and twelve year olds had developed, to varying degrees, into a highly discerning news audience. Many had become much more aware of how journalism works and how it constructs the world in particular (preferred) ways. Involvement in the project had also resulted in participants' wider engagement with the news, with many regularly tuning into radio news bulletins, television news and reading newspapers that came into their homes. The more aware they became of how the news is put together, the issues that are routinely included and those that are not, the more they tended to question what they were being told and how. *First Edition*, many indicated, presented the news in an engaging, challenging, non-patronising, and yet accessible style. Moreover, its use of respected Channel 4 journalist, Jon Snow, as anchor (alongside a child co-anchor) indicated to them that the producers were taking them seriously as an audience. CBBC *Newsround*'s perceived use of young, sometimes overly-animated 'down with the kids' presenters, tended to be regarded by this group as patronising; they were of the view that the programme was insufficiently challenging for the child news audience. In contrast, pupils in another class at Hillhead Primary (and those we spoke to at a different primary school in the city) were unaware of the existence of *First Edition*, so had nothing to compare to in presenting their assessments of *Newsround*. Many of these children thought *Newsround* did a fairly good job in covering the news, and most did not follow the news, in general, to the same extent as the *First Edition* group.

We concluded that the more children are exposed to the news and challenged to engage with it in a stimulating and supportive learning environment, the more likely they are to become discerning news audiences. Despite adult concern that the news is often too frightening for children, and therefore that there is a need to protect them from it, most *First Edition* project pupils were not upset or traumatised by the events of 9/11 nor its reporting (of course, living, far from the events, in Scotland, might have had something do with it). Instead, many expressed sadness for those who had lost loved ones whilst also indicating their desire to have more information with which to understand what happened and why. Participation in the letter-writing project seems to have produced what we referred to as the "*First Edition* effect". If the news is presented to children in formats that are challenging but also accessible, then the more children may come to know about the world and feel less overwhelmed by events. In an enabling learning environment where children are able to interact with each other and with adults, including news producers who are keen to develop a more interactive relationship with their audiences, the more likely children are to develop critical news literacy and thus become more active citizens.

How might academics, children's news producers, schools and young audiences build on the insights garnered from this type of research to contribute to the young audience's engagement with news? What sort of balance might be struck between concerns around the possible negative emotional effects of the news on children and a desire to enhance children's critical news literacy?

Issue 2
Children and citizenship
Case Study: BBC/Arts and Humanities Research Council
Knowledge Exchange Project: BBC Newsround

Several years ago, I helped to develop an AHRC/BBC Knowledge Exchange pilot project examining the ways in which children were engaging with *Newsround* in an age of digital media.[3] We set out to determine what children aged nine to fifteen wanted from the programme (though it should be noted that *Newsround*'s target audience is eight to twelve year olds), and how well it connected with them as citizens. The project also provided an opportunity to explore how academic/producer partnerships might enrich research insights. The collaboration proved to be an exciting and fruitful one. The main output was the 2009 report, *What do Children Want from the BBC? Children's Content and Participatory Environments in an Age of Citizen Media* (Carter, Messenger Davies, Allan, Mendes, Milani and Wass 2009).

Commenting on the significance of academic/media professional research collaborations, one of our BBC partners, Roy Milani, highlighted, in his foreword to the report, what he believed both parties stood to gain:

> I was very keen to see how academic research would help to inform us as programme makers and content producers. I was particularly interested to see how this approach would allow us to understand our child news audiences in ways that traditional audience research might not. I have to say I was not disappointed. In adopting innovative research methods alongside traditional techniques, and by using an academic, analytical approach to the resulting data, some very interesting findings emerged. Some of them confirmed what had already been understood from previous audience research undertaken by the BBC, but there were critical areas where important new insights into to children's attitudes and behaviours emerged.
>
> Some of the areas which were of particular interest to me and which are highlighted in the project report are:
>
> • the relationship between linear TV and web usage
> • the importance of news from all UK nations in children's news provision
> • how targeting age groups is critical and how some are underserved
> • the desire of the child news audience to contribute in tangible ways to output and content
> (Carter et al. 2009: 3)

I'll mention just a few recommendations coming out of the study which are pertinent to questions around the role children's news producers might play in sustaining children's citizenship:

- Producers working with children and young people should be encouraged to question their own assumptions about how children relate to the news
- Children indicated that Newsround represents a unique and important space where their ideas and opinions are seen to be important. As such, Newsround should ensure that its news provision supports and also challenges young people in their development as young citizens. Producers should not avoid addressing a wide range of political, social, economic and personal issues, as they can always be addressed in ways that are relevant and appropriate to the child audience
- [...] A significant number of older children strongly supported the development of a dedicated news provision for the young teenager audience

(Carter et al. 2009: 37-38)

With this final recommendation in mind, we made a bid for further funding from the AHRC/BBC, through its Knowledge Infusion scheme, to examine the prospect of developing a news provision for the 'transitional audience' (twelve to fifteen year olds). In our first study, many in this age group told us that they felt too old for *Newsround* and too young for adult news (the latter often regarded as incomprehensible, boring or exclusionary of young people's opinions and experiences).

Issue 3
Teen news
Case Study: BBC/Arts and Humanities Research Council
Knowledge Infusion Project

Having obtained funding for a follow-up study, we set out to explore whether young people supported the idea of a dedicated news service for teenagers and, if so, what it might look like.[4] We asked our contacts at the five secondary schools from the first study to select one group of Year 7 students (Year 8 in Scotland, where it is the first year of secondary school) who actively follow the news; pupils were aged eleven to thirteen. In our fieldwork at the schools, we invited pupils to offer their comments on the idea of a BBC teen news service. Most were in favour, maintaining that many young people are very interested in what is going on in the world, and not just in popular culture, as adults seemed to assume. We then asked them to imagine themselves as a team of independent news producers seeking a commission from the BBC for the development of such a service (we posed as representatives of the BBC). Along with our BBC partner, we had developed a 'pitch sheet' that the pupils used to outline their ideas, to include the service's name, typical contents, platforms, scheduling, frequency, and distribution.

After leaving them to brainstorm for 45 minutes, we asked them to choose one of their team to pitch the idea to us.

Pupils demonstrated much enthusiasm for a teen news service, citing its potential to enhance a sense of civic belonging and its value in confirming that adults regarded teens' opinions and contributions to society as important. Groups offered a broad range of suggestions regarding delivery platforms, including television and radio news bulletins, online news, and news magazines. Content should include regional news, basic forms of interactivity online and in broadcast news (such as 'Have your Say' and 'i-debate'), offer a mix of good and bad news, and fun and serious topics. Presenters on television and radio would be teens or young people in their twenties. Broadcast news services ought to be regular, prominent (on BBC One) and in prime time.

We also gave pupils a short questionnaire to gain further insights into their news consumption habits. Although it was a small sample (26 pupils), so not generalisable to this population of young people, what they told us is nevertheless interesting and valuable in considering the likely views of this age group. For instance, most said that their primary source of news is television. Research evidence, including our own, has consistently confirmed that television news is the most popular format for young teens. Pupils in our study said they typically turn to the internet for gaming and social media rather than for news. It is worth noting that Ofcom's 2013 report, *Children and Parents: Media Use and Attitudes Report*, confirms that television remains the favoured medium for news with this age group. That said, in our study, the pupils in our study offered creative suggestions for improving web news provision for teens, including greater awareness of the broad array of topics and issues of interest to them.

There is clearly an urgent need for the BBC to listen to what young teens might want from a news service. At the moment there appears to be little consultation taking place with them, resulting in sometimes rather specious assumptions being made about how best to reach them (if, indeed, at all). Since television is still the most widely accessible and used platform for news, any service would have to include television as a means of content delivery. The BBC should continue to produce factual television content that takes children seriously: *Newsround* is the obvious example, but thoughtful consideration must also be given to developing services for twelve to fifteen year olds. If the BBC concludes that is important to draw young people to news websites, then producers need to be aware of where young people are already going online. This would mean undertaking research about the most popular online sites with this age group in order to create links with them to any BBC news provision for young teens.

Conclusions

In its most recent service licence for CBBC (2013), the BBC Trust lays out its commitment to sustaining children's civic life: "through its news, current affairs and factual output and through content reflecting social engagement, citizenship and life skills" (2013: 4). This important pledge ought to apply not only to CBBC's target audience of six to twelve year olds, but to older children as well. It would be rather unfair to assume that the BBC should have sole responsibility for this endeavour. It is my hope, therefore, that organisations such as the Children's Media Foundation, in collaboration with others, might facilitate the formation of strategic alliances between media academics, producers, regulators, schools and young people to encourage innovative thinking about how best to advance young citizens' critical news literacy skills and civic empowerment.

References

Bazalgette, C., Harkand, J., and James, C. (2008) *Lifeblood of Democracy? Learning about Broadcast News*. A BFI Report for Ofcom. http://stakeholders.ofcom.org.uk/binaries/research/media-literacy/lifeblood.pdf

BBC Trust (2013) *CBBC Service Licence* http://downloads.bbc.co.uk/bbctrust/assets/files/pdf/regulatory_framework/service_licences/tv/2013/cbbc_sep13.pdf

Carter, C., Messenger Davies, M., Allan, S., Mendes, K., Milani, R., and Wass, L. (2009) *What do Children Want from the BBC? Children's Content and Participatory Environments in and Age of Citizen Media*. AHRC/BBC Knowledge Exchange Report. http://www.bbc.co.uk/blogs/knowledgeexchange/cardifftwo.pdf

Ofcom (2013) *Children and Parents: Media Use and Attitudes Report*. http://stakeholders.ofcom.org.uk/binaries/research/media-literacy/october-2013/research07Oct2013.pdf

Vale, P. (2014) Newsnight: Alain de Botton asks 'What's the Point of News?'; Huffington Post, 29 January (http://www.huffingtonpost.co.uk/2014/01/29/newsnight-alain-de-botton-news_n_4691031.html)

Endnotes

1 MeCCSA is a professional association representing UK media, communication and cultural studies academics.

2 The *First Edition* project team consisted of Cynthia Carter, Máire Messenger Davies, and Karin Wahl-Jorgensen, Cardiff University, and Stuart Allan, then at the University of the West of England.

3 The project included fieldwork (2007-2008) in Bournemouth, Cardiff, Coleraine, and Glasgow with over 200 children and young people. In addition to myself, colleagues on the project were Stuart Allan (then at Bournemouth University), Máire Messenger Davies (University of Ulster). Roy Milani and Louise Wass (BBC). The research assistant was Kaitlynn Mendes (Cardiff University). We would like to thank the BBC/ARHC Knowledge Exchange Programme that funded this and the follow up Knowledge Infusion projects.

4 In the second study, our BBC partner was former *Newsround* producer Ian Prince.

Making Sense of the Research
The CMF's Parent Portal

17

Colin Ward

A brief search online will quickly identify some fairly esoteric research projects. For example, a 2005 paper written by Victor Breno Meyer-Rochow of International University, Bremen, and Jozsef Gal of Lorand Eotvos University, Hungary, calculated the pressure that builds up inside a penguin prior to defecation: 'Pressures Produced When Penguins Poo: Calculations On Avian Defecation'. Spanish researchers A. Mulet, J. Benedito and J. Bon of the Polytechnic University of Valencia, wrote in 2006 about the ultrasonic velocity in cheddar cheese as affected by temperature. (Why didn't they pick Manchego or a creamy Catalonian mató?)

I'm sure those research projects have value, but I think most of us would struggle to appreciate their significance at first glance. That is not the case with research into children's media; there is a keen interest in how children experience and interact with their media. Parents are drawn, irresistibly, towards every burst of media panic around the publication – or, in the case of many news reports, the rediscovery – of a research project that claims, for example, to identify the ideal number of hours of screen time for children under four. Politicians and policy makers look for research to help them analyse complex issues around industry regulation, online safety, and the role of media technology in education. Even stressed-out media producers will occasionally turn away from their Sisyphean task and freewheel for a brief moment during the production cycle, taking time to talk to academics about how children respond to the TV programmes, apps, games, and interactive websites they are creating.

That is why one of the objectives of the CMF is to support research into children's media and to disseminate the results of that research to parents, policy makers, and the press. This year we took a step towards achieving that with the launch of the 'Parent Portal' on the CMF's website, an area designed to help parents make sense of the wide range of research currently available, both good and bad. The starting point for the project was a survey of parents, followed up with focus group research, conducted for the CMF by the Dubit research agency in Leeds. The research identified six questions that are of particular interest to parents and we took those as our starting point for deciding which research papers to highlight.

The questions that most concerned parents were focused around the impact of children's media habits on their social life and development, an area that is notoriously hard to research. Many of our own supporters make the valid point that questions about the impact of media on children's lives are impossible to answer. But we did not want to duck the issue. It is clear that parents are concerned about these issues and are also confused by the way the research is reported in the media, and we felt we had to tackle the debate head on. The CMF commissioned Professor Lydia Plowman of the University of Edinburgh to produce an overview of current research that would at least begin to provide partial answers to the questions parents are asking.

So what are the questions? Here is the full list:

> What sort of media might be 'bad' for my children?
> Will playing violent video games make my child more aggressive?
> Will spending too much time in front of a screen affect my child's social skills?
> What are the possible risks associated with my child going online?
> Will spending too much time in front of a screen affect my child's education?
> Should I be concerned about the range of content available to children?

To reiterate the point, we appreciate that some of these questions are almost impossible to answer within the constraints of ethical research. We have tried to make that point clear to parents and we have also acknowledged the limits of research. The Parent Portal attempts to give answers where possible, and explains why it is impossible to answer the question when that is the case.

We have also tried to suggest there may be other questions we could ask of researchers that might be more fruitful. In our summary for the question about the impact of violent video games on children's behaviour, we acknowledge there is research, mainly from the United States, suggesting a statistical link between some video games and higher levels of anger and aggression, but we also point out there is no evidence for any causal link. We emphasise that much of this research has been questioned and that no one has ever proven a link between a video game and any act of violence in the real world. And to balance out the summary, we also reference studies that suggest certain video games may increase pro-social behaviour.

We hope that this approach will help to balance the debate. The TV was the first 'screen' to enter the home and since then we have been subjected to a steady stream of negative reports on the impact of screen time on children. Despite the fact that the published research makes it clear the impact of screen time is far more nuanced, media reporting has always focused on references to the potential for a negative impact.

When, on the Parent Portal, we address the question of the impact of screen time, we emphasise the difficulties of conducting research and point out that some researchers are forced to make assumptions.

For example, we explain that some of the figures given for children's screen time are based on parents' estimates, which makes it hard to gather accurate information. We also ask parents to think about what we mean by screen time; if a toddler is playing with toys in the living room and the TV is on, does that count as screen time? And how do you measure screen time in a modern home when more than one screen may be in use at the same time?

Of course, the risk of pointing out the complexities of research is that we will leave parents even more confused and isolated. We have tried to address that by offering some practical advice, based on research, which may help parents develop new strategies to work with their children's media habits, instead of feeling they have to fight against them.

Our hope is that the tone of these web pages will raise the quality of the debate around children's media and encourage parents to see these questions in a different light. As we all know, there are no simple or definitive answers and it is highly unlikely research can ever provide them. But that does not imply that we should not be concerned about the type of media content children are consuming. We are trying to shift the debate onto more realistic territory and encourage parents to make their own judgements about their child's media habits, based on their assessment of specific media content and the way their own, highly individual, child is likely to respond to that content.

Making Money Out of Children ⑱

Mark Sorrell

Children make annoying noises

At the beginning of this discussion and the end of the day, the biggest problem with the issue of monetising children is that it *starts* with, "Won't you think of the children?!"

It's a technique usually employed by such august truth-seekers as *The Daily Mail*, thrown in at the end of an otherwise losing battle, or used to crowbar in actions that would seem sinister without the child-sized fig leaf (internet filters, anyone?). Mixing together money and children is guaranteed to get us off to a sentimental start. Even those of us that make our money mixing those exact things.

I'm a freemium game design and behaviour change consultant, or to use my official title 'EVIL MAN'. For the past two years, at the Children's Media Conference, I've stood up on stage and talked about extracting money from children. I've talked about ways of doing it that aren't evil or silly or bad and how the concerns many people were expressing about apps for kids, and especially free to play apps, appeared to be a mixture of moral panic, horrifyingly legitimate horror, and well-honed ignorance.

And it's still a big concern; in fact it's quite clearly getting bigger. Both the EU and the OFT have been looking at this question and, while they seem unlikely to take to the industry with a stick, there's no question that the days of wild west liberties and devil-may-care attitudes to the digitisation of removing money from children are basically over.

But while we can't carry on quite as we were, we can't go back to how things used to be, either. Free is the price point that many apps, if not most, will continue to be sold at. Kids will continue to ask their parents for digital games and apps, along with the more familiar brightly coloured plastic things; fuzzy, furry things; and things that make incredibly annoying noises.

So where are things going to go? And what should those who want to make their money from entertaining children really be doing to ensure they're both behaving respectfully and making lots of lovely money?

Children are badly paid

We've been comfortable about making money out of children for as long as we've had children and money, In fact it's not that long since 'making money out of children' had more to do with how far you could stick one up a chimney than how many Moshlings were needed to stop them from screaming for more than an eighth of a second.

Of course monetising children isn't about monetising children at all. Children don't have any money. They have access to money, sure, but it is their parents' money, not their own. Children are, on the whole, very badly paid.

So when we ask these questions, really we're often asking much stranger ones, such as, "How much should we let companies use children as tiny, poorly-behaved salespeople inserted deep into customers' homes?" and "Should we be angry that someone invented a new way for children to steal off their parents?" and "How old do children need to be until we explain that gambling is a thing that totally exists, and is really fun, and also really bad?"

To start to answer this question in any sort of meaningful way, we need to be asking how we use the best traits of modern media forms to create great products for children; how we educate parents into understanding how things can be better than they used to be; and how the commercial realities of modern marketplaces can be used to create commercial models that work for everyone.

Children beat you at games

Children are learning machines. That's what they do. They start out knowing absolutely nothing, and then somehow, through a process of putting things in their mouths, hitting things, and shouting, they become accountants and race car drivers and the person that invented golf.

Games are teaching machines. They are machines that proffer an inscrutable black box, in which they hold their rules and systems, and invite the player to investigate what those rules and systems might be, by using the tools the game also – very thoughtfully – provides. Players start out knowing absolutely nothing and end up being chess grandmasters or doing any number of incredible things in *Minecraft* that I could link to if this were the internet and not a book. Google it or something?

When running a test on a new game I was developing for four year olds, I asked a friend with a child of appropriate age – in this case three – to video herself playing the game with him. At the start of the video, she interrupts the child from what he was doing to play this simple game. What he was doing, was playing *Sonic Adventure 2* on the PlayStation 3. In literacy terms, that's like asking him to put down Harry Potter so she could go through a Mr Men book with him.

This is not unusual. Video games are an incredibly perfect fit for children's minds. Teaching machines for learning machines. Somehow we, as adults, decided we should not explore games immediately and with great force, because games are sort of strange, and kind of fun, and a bit new, and full of loud colours and bright noises. Children will gain from videogames and seek out videogames and want videogames and demand videogames. And videogames will teach them. It's up to us to decide what they teach, but aside from that, the battle, such as it may have been considered a battle at all, is well and truly lost.

Games will be the great teaching method of the future, because they're the great teaching method of the present. We just keep letting school get in the way.

Children enjoy plastic objects

So games are something children love and need and can benefit from and that's the end of that. But what about that freemium business? What about that bit where you get people to pay for stuff in the game using horrible manipulation and devious trickery, and holding people by the ankles and shaking them until money falls out of their pockets?

Well there are a few issues here. Freemium apps aimed exclusively at kids are actually pretty rare and, thanks to a number of high profile missteps, certainly not getting any more popular. A look at the top kids' apps charts reveals that, rather uniquely, the top grossing apps are paid and not free. That's definitely not true of the adult-orientated categories. The hubbub of the past two years has worked, and the kids market has largely got its house in order.

The problem comes when kids play games that are aimed at adults, but that children also adore. We've already established that kids love games and can deal with game mechanics that are at a far greater level of complexity than they exhibit in other areas of their development.

Here they do sit cheek by jowl with the freemium model and its potential for creating middle-England foaming-mouthed headlines. But once again, we shouldn't leap to bared-teeth conclusions. Most developers still don't really understand how the model works. It is, after all, pretty counter-intuitive, and simply copying what another developer is doing, without understanding why, will often either not work at all, or create unpleasant side-effects and perverse incentives.

But there is a gradual understanding that within freemium, it's not the more mercenary and mendacious techniques that are the most successful. A well designed freemium game uses money as a way to increase player agency and allow an extra form of expression rather than as a gating mechanic or devious trick. Spending money in many of the more successful freemium games is a symbol of the player's enjoyment, not capitulation.

And when it comes to children interacting with these games, well, it's not like we haven't historically been teaching kids to say, gamble, anyway. Panini Sticker books, those are definitely gambling for kids, and they sell six billion stickers a year. Those little LEGO Minifigure packs with a random minifig are gambling for kids. LEGO are the world's biggest toy company. A closed packet containing a random prize has been an acceptable way to stop a child from making terrible, horrible noises in a public place for decades.

And they are also infinitely more exciting than a known prize! Until you open them, and they don't contain the particular plastic object you wanted more than your own head, and then they are rubbish. Except the particular plastic object you wanted is still the greatest object since energy first became matter, so why not buy another one and see if this time you get lucky?

But you are not so lucky.

It's a lesson that needs to be learned. Better it is learned now with a plastic fireman than later with a mortgage payment, eh?

Children learn disappointment gradually

Our acceptance of these physical goods and physical transactions over the mysterious and otherworldly 'in-app purchase' (IAP) is surely clear to see. The stickers and LEGO are fully within the control of the parent and easy to understand because you can hold them and hide them and throw them at the cat. An IAP is... well what is it exactly that you just bought? Some berries or gold or a different coloured imaginary dragon? How can that be worth anything? What on earth is going on? Someone, somewhere is definitely having a laugh.

But this is where freemium games might actually be harnessed to do some good. Money is becoming more and more virtual every day and we have a duty to bring our children up to understand how to deal with that world. It's pleasing and simple to see a transaction existing in the form of your heavy, strange-smelling metal discs in exchange for their interestingly shaped sugar, but that is not the way the world is going. Money is becoming more and more virtual. A number on a computer screen, not a bit of metal or piece of paper with a picture of a lady on.

A look at Bitcoin, and further into the weird world of crypto-currencies (particularly the barking mad Dogecoin) shows that currencies themselves are becoming less predictable or safe or comprehensible, using our traditional ways of thinking. Money is becoming something new and it won't mean the same thing to your children as it did to you. That's never really been true for any previous generation.

And the things we buy with our strange new money, based on weird new currencies, aren't real things, and often aren't even ours to keep. The concept of possession itself is dwindling. Look at Airbnb and Uber, Netflix and Zipcar. We don't buy, we rent. We stream, we share, we sustain. We don't really have much choice; after all, we've sort of used up rather a lot of the world's resources already. Our children are growing into this world, of digital and transient and passage, and it is this world that we must prepare them for.

So the place where children's entertainment is heading, where monetisation is heading, is not a problem – it is a challenge. Giving children access to more meaningful budgeting experiences is entirely possible. Letting parents control the funds their children have and let them learn how to spend them is an opportunity to create a more financially savvy generation. And that's an opportunity we shouldn't miss out on. Teaching children about the world they are going to inhabit is a duty, a commercial opportunity and a creative challenge. We should be relishing that.

It's a rather better choice than pretending games are stupid or teaching kids about the joys of gambling, don't you think?

My Children are Your Children

Gary Pope

Shakespeare was a right one for dads. Prospero, Lear and Shylock. All the greats. Sort of. Maybe it was because he was a bit of an absentee-dad himself (too busy having a knees-up and bear-bating in Southwark) that he wrote in *The Merchant of Venice*: "It is a wise father that knows his own child". So true.

It's really hard work being a good dad. It's not like anyone actually tells you what to do, is it? Indeed it's always seemed a bit of a shame to me that it was actually an uncle that said, "With great power comes great responsibility". Because it's truer of a dad than of perhaps anything else.

Except maybe the creator of content for children.

We share a very small part of the responsibility for the effective development of my children, you and me. It's the bit when I'm not there and the children are experiencing your stuff. It could be whilst reading a book, it might be when they are playing with a toy or swiping and tapping at a touchscreen, it could even be whilst watching a TV show (yes, children still do that). I am not always there when you are, so I'm going to trust you to do the right thing.

Only it's not that simple, is it? You've got a business to run.

It could be said that many children spend more time with their media than they do their fathers. In our media drenched world without schedules, being always tuned-in and never dropping out (unless you're on BT Infinity) means we, as parents and content creators, have even more of a responsibility to know our children than our own parents and predecessors did us. Because, like it or not, my children are partly a product of your creation.

So, as a dad I've got a right to stand on my child-protecting soapbox and hector. So... without any sort of data set and a focus group of, ermmm, two, here goes...

Let's start with the telly. The phrase 'Children's TV Channel' has become a bit of a misnomer in our house. I asked my children Laurence and Daisy what their favourite TV channels were – each, without a moment's hesitation, said Netflix. It's not on TV (unless you've got a pricey Smart one) and it's not a channel. But if you're five or ten it's both of these things.

Netflix is a great experience. It knows what you like and it doesn't matter whether you're on your computer or your dad's; you get your stuff served up nice and quickly. And if you have to stop for some inconvenience like going to school, you don't need to make sure you've set the PVR (how archaic): you just log back in, click on the show you were watching and off you go. And they don't serve up stuff that is 'on brand' for the 'channel'. Nope. You get something for everyone and given that children have never ever been channel-loyal and instead give preference to specific shows, it's a televisual smorgasbord.

Netflix is winning because we live in the Experience Economy. There's no question that what our children expect is a seamless fluid experience: so much so that we get quite put out when the user experience (UX) – on whatever platform – isn't quite where we thought it ought to be. They've never had it so good but then, they've never known any different.

It's a first class brand experience that has single-handedly replaced the Children's TV channel as the media weapon of choice for the under twelves. And it took them only about eighteen months. The raft of subscription video-on-demand (SVOD) platforms or services targeting children is getting a bit silly now – but here's the thing – why would you pay more than six pounds per month for subscription services when actually this one does it for the whole family? Interesting times ahead…

The one thing we do know about the children's media landscape that isn't changing is the interconnectedness it has with commerce. Ultimately content has to be paid for by someone, somewhere. Unless you're insanely gifted and write a very good grant application you're going to need to think about the toys. And perhaps even the underpants. Laurence loves underpants. And he loves dinosaurs and he especially loves stories. Little surprise then that a favourite book of his is *Dinosaurs Love Underpants*. And it's a corker.

That's a bit of background.

Last night he wants some bedtime stories on the iPad. It's not news to you that incredible things have been happening in our world on this most child-friendly of devices. Great companies are doing great things and some of the big boys in the playground are even going beyond the colour of the money (to a degree) in making some great story apps that have genuine value.

Given Laurence's love of underpants I thought I'd do a search. Turns out there are a veritable drawer full from Simon and Schuster. So I spend $10.00 – that's £5.99 in old money – for, wait for it… *Aliens in Underpants Save the World*. Laurence happens to think he's half alien so this is manna from heaven for him.

Same author, same illustrator, similar story to *Dinosaurs Love Underpants* but set in space. With bigger pants.

Underpants, spaceships and aliens that save the world? We can't go wrong.

But we do.

Or rather they do.

Let me explain…

Laurence was happy with the whole experience – I did the voices; he got to swipe the pages. Nice story. Laurence went to sleep happily dreaming of how his brother aliens (he was insistent they were his brothers) saved the world from a rogue comet intent on planetary annihilation by creating a huge shield of sewn together underpants. What could be better? Happy days.

But not for me.

I've been cheated. I just paid £5.99 ($10.00 in new money) for a digital flipbook. A very bad digital flip book. The code didn't play nicely with the device and so I was incessantly spinning the iPad. It hadn't been reformatted to fit the screen properly and there was a rubbish letterbox effect.

I was smarting by the end by being digitally burned.

But Laurence was happy, so does any of this matter? You bet it does. I just can't get my head around how the proper book can sell for £3.99 but the virtual one (which is little more than a badly saved PDF) costs £5.99. No interactivity – no sound, no cheeky little 'Easter eggs' hiding away longing for father and son to serendipitously discover them together. Not even an alien's fart. Nothing but a badly drawn PDF.

What a shame that this very, very good book has been so let down by the very commerce that is its industry's lifeblood. I've always thought that the publishing industry would colonise the children's media landscape: they have a ready-made audience from the books, and clever people to make it happen, and a conscientiousness that puts those licensing people to shame. But what I was missing was the brand thing. Publishing companies, with one or two clear exceptions, have not made the jump to the hyperspace of the new branded universe very easily.

In these tough times which is more important: the quarterly return or nurturing and developing long-term relationships with your consumers? I will never buy another digital book from them again. Ever. And I'll tell my friends not to bother either. Lots of them. If I had them.

I bought it from iBooks so I should have known better. But this is 2014. My expectations are high and for $10.00 they are very high. And there's this other thing that still needs to be ironed out… when is a book an app? And when is an app a book? I thought we'd worked all that out at the last CMC.

For children, convergence is the continuity of storytelling. They do not differentiate between platforms whether invented by Gutenberg or Jobs. It doesn't matter as long as it's a great story well delivered. This wasn't well delivered.

When you buy a 'digital book' for children on a tablet you buy a story experience. It's just the way it is. You could argue that Laurence enjoyed the story experience so the rest doesn't matter.

And you'd be right.

But just think what he didn't get from the experience that he could have. Especially for that money. And it wasn't just this book. I downloaded three others just to see. Great stories, rubbish experiences.

Bottom line? I felt ripped off. That my underpants, never mind the shirt on my back, had been ripped from me. And that's about as big a sin as a marketer can deliver.

But there is a bigger one. One that goes even beyond not providing a fair value exchange in terms of cash given for experience received.

And that's putting shareholder value before moral responsibility. Mattel bought Megabrands for a bazillion dollars. Good strategic move. They're never going to build a construction business from scratch. Mega Bloks tends to pick up the licenses that LEGO doesn't want or need. *Halo*, Moshi and *Call of Duty* for example. And they make some really nice product.

What troubles me about this specifically is that *Call of Duty*, the game, is a PEGI 18. That PEGI rating means it's not suitable for people under the age of eighteen.

Yes, Mega Bloks do dutifully put 10+ on the construction toy packs. And some sets actually have 12+ but the fact is these are toys for boys 7+. These are toys that are heavily branded and will drive the children to the parent brand which isn't for seven year olds and is the scourge of primary schools everywhere. It's Call of (Bloody) Duty. Literally.

This is arbitrary age profiling to maximize return and reality says that, in the connected world, these kinds of construction toys are only going to sell more copies of the game. Or the game will be borrowed in the playground from kids that have got older brothers and sisters.

So, what the gaming, toy and licensing industries all appear to be saying is that it's OK to sell toys for media franchises that are 18+ as long as the toys can be made for ten year olds. Nonsense. Laurence asked for a set and he's five. Because the toys are cool. And as construction toys go they are very, very cool. I've got an Xbox – so he's going to be asking for the game next. And that's not happening so I have to say no to one iteration of this brand but could say yes to another; and that, if you're a digital native like Laurence, is really weird. And if you're a dad it's a pain in the backside. You're not helping me here.

I care about the commercial imperative here because it is wrong. Not commercially of course. It makes perfect sense. In fact it's great marketing.

But we're talking about children. Children that live in a joined-up, cross-platform and transmedia world. Don't make them want the big thing through enabling them to have the little things when the big thing is something that they should not have access to until they are old enough.

There's a reason the game is rated 18+.

Someone is being very, very naughty and not taking their responsibilities to their consumers seriously enough. Though they do a very good job at the other end with Skylanders. Though I'm not sure they understand who their audience really are, actually. Or is it that they do and there's more dollars to be had by conveniently tempting the children into buying the big ticket games through the Trojan horse of construction blocks? Either way they're missing the point.

The point of all family targeted marketing – comms, product and experience - is to get past the gatekeeper (me and Mrs P) to the end consumer (Daisy and Laurence) and to make the gatekeepers feel good about it too. There's nothing we like more than seeing our children genuinely happy. And if we have to invest in some product then that's absolutely fine. We'll like you for it.

And this where your creativity can make a remarkable contribution to this co-parenting malarkey. This is where I really need you to parent with me: the characters and narratives the children see on screen define who they are and who they want to be; they model behaviours and they help show children how to socialise.

This is Laurence with his friend. Laurence has got the hat on. Laurence is from Crystal Palace, a suburb overlooking the city of London from the highest point in South London on the nearside of Sydenham Hill.

Laurence's friend is five too and is from a small township called 'The Location' that nestles on a beautiful hillside overlooking the Atlantic ocean about 60 miles around the coast from Cape Town, South Africa. It's called 'The Location' because that's where the black community was settled back in the day.

The two boys met in the play park by the beach on New Year's day. Laurence only speaks English. His friend only Xhosa. The first language of Nelson Mandela. They played and they played and they played.

They played for so long and they played so well that I managed to read the paper. There was an article about the supposed conflict in the Mandela family over who should take control of the Mandela 'brand'.

I looked up, a little saddened, and Laurence and his friend were still playing. After 90 minutes it was time to go.

As we walked home I asked him what his friend's name was. "Me and my friend don't speak the same language and I couldn't understand what he said his name was."

"But you need to know what your friend's name is, Laurence." I said.

"No, not really. As long as you play nicely it doesn't matter what your names are or if you speak different languages. As long as you're friends that's all that really matters, Dad."

OK.

"So what did you play?"

"Stuff."

"What stuff?"

"Just running and stuff."

"For 90 minutes?"

"Yeah."

Kids don't need the toys or any item from the multitude of categories you have to sell out to in order make a profit. What they need are opportunities to learn, grow and socialise. And I think this is what you make – not apps, or TV shows or toys or books but experiences and memories that contribute to the happy, successful and effective development of my (our) children.

And that means putting them front and centre of all your thinking. Just like every good marketer should do.

And if you do that we'll love buying the toys. And books. And apps. And even the bloody underpants.

What's New in Children's Apps **20**
Stuart Dredge

2014 is already an exciting year for innovative, beautiful, creative and/or educational new children's apps, but the caveat before writing about them is this: just because parents see them in that way doesn't mean their children will.

Parents buy apps, but children use them, and what appeals to the former isn't always to the tastes of the latter, as I thought when trying to persuade my increasingly grumpy four year old of the merits of a marvellous Montessori maths app when he just wanted to make 'Talking Tom Cat' squeakily repeat the word 'bottom'…

People still marvel at the idea of two year olds who can use iPads, but we perhaps don't talk enough about the way those two year olds will turn into four and five year olds determined to use the apps THEY like rather than what their parents like, and seven or eight year olds keen to make their own choices on the app stores, rather than rely on adults as filters.

In short, you can fill a device with those innovative, beautiful, creative and/or educational apps, but you can't make children use them. What follows are some trends I've spotted around what's being developed for kids, but I'd stop short of suggesting they're always reflective of what's actually being used in volume.

Still, 2014 is an exciting year. One trend fuelling that excitement is the idea of kids as creators: not just passively consuming entertainment through apps, but drawing, animating, storytelling and crafting. Born makers.

In recent times, I've loved the way 'Sago Mini Doodlecast' gets kids to talk while drawing pictures and records both to make storytelling videos; the way 'Night Zookeeper Teleporting Torch' sparks their creative instincts around the theme of magical animals and the format of daily drawing missions; and the way 'Mr Shingu's Paper Zoo' and its sequel 'Paper Ocean' turn digital origami into engaging games.

I'm intrigued by the idea of digital apps creating physical objects. At the whizzy end of the scale, there are apps like 'Blokify' and 'Monstermatic' which turn kids' on-screen creations into 3D printed objects (ordered and sent in the post for children who don't have access to a 3D printer at home – i.e. 99.9999999 per cent of them).

'Draw My Doll' offers a more crafty take on that idea: touchscreen paintings turned into hand-sewn dolls, while 'Foldify Zoo' creates virtual animals that parents can then print out to fold together in the real world. And 'Squigglefish' and 'Drawnimal' offer different takes on getting an app to interact with pencil 'n' paper drawings. These are all apps I'd like to shout about when people suggest that screen time can't be creative.

It's a short leap from creativity to crafting, and no discussion of what kids are doing with apps in 2014 could be complete without hailing *Minecraft*. Developer Mojang's crafting game has sold 21m copies on smartphones and tablets, and I'd be willing to bet a significant portion of those sales have gone to children (albeit often through their parents).

You could fill several books with the wonderful things happening in and around *Minecraft* and children. In 2014, I think more parents and teachers are understanding the culture and creativity of *Minecraft*, and its expressive and/or educational potential. Their interest, support and ideas could fuel more fun ahead.

Another trend that should be talked about a bit more this year – in the television industry especially – is that children aren't just playing *Minecraft*, they're watching other people playing it. *Minecraft* videos have become one of the most popular categories on YouTube, with billions of views. A lot of those views are coming from a) kids and b) mobile devices.

The Sky Does Minecraft channel has 9.8m subscribers and 1.9bn lifetime views. Yogscast has 6.9m subscribers and 2.5bn lifetime views. Stampy has 2.6m subscribers and 1bn lifetime views. And earlier this year Stampy's creator, Joseph Garrett, announced plans to launch a second channel focused on education.

Watch the latter carefully: YouTube is now a place where a young British gamer pretending to be a cartoon cat exploring *Minecraft* is an edutainment brand as relevant as *Sesame Street* or CBeebies. That's fascinating, and provokes the question of whether linear TV channels should be finding a place for creators like Garrett and *Minecraft* culture, or whether this content's natural home is on YouTube.

YouTube *Minecraft* channels are examples of 'new networks' for – and the definition is increasingly loose – children's television. There are other examples. AwesomenessTV is a YouTube multi-channel network (MCN) focusing on tweens and teens, and owned by DreamWorks Animation.

Other MCNs are incubating musicians, comedians, fashionistas and personalities who are as popular with many children as anyone they discover through traditional media. Elsewhere in the online video world, Netflix and Amazon are commissioning slates of original children's programming – much of

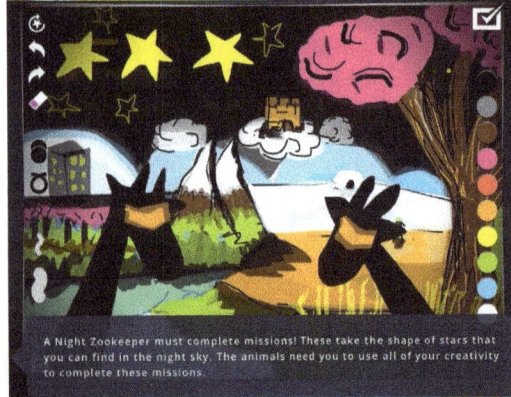

A Night Zookeeper must complete missions! These take the shape of stars that you can find in the night sky. The animals need you to use all of your creativity to complete these missions.

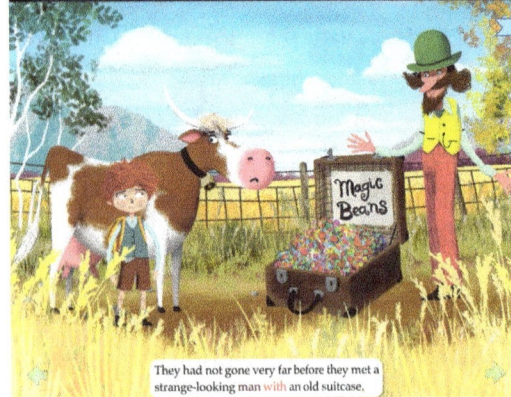

They had not gone very far before they met a strange-looking man with an old suitcase.

which will be watched on tablets (or watched on bigger screens controlled by tablets) by their young audiences.

More new networks? It sounds strange to talk of anything *Angry Birds* related as under the radar, but Rovio's development of its ToonsTV network – delivered partly through its *Angry Birds* games but also now online – into a distribution channel for more than just its own *Angry Birds Toons* is fascinating to watch. 2 billion views since its launch in March 2013 is the start of something potentially much bigger, if kids' interest in the brand doesn't flag over the next twelve to eighteen months.

Another apps trend I'd flag up is actually a familiar idea to anyone working in children's entertainment: kids respond to strong characters. The trend is that they can increasingly find them in apps as well as TV shows, books and games. 'Clumsy Ninja' isn't even a game specifically for children, but its endearingly goofy hero with his raggy doll physics has huge potential in other forms of entertainment, if its creator NaturalMotion – bought by social games giant Zynga for $527m in January – so desires.

Toca Boca is already one of the most well known children's app brands for parents, and all its apps are character-led – albeit with no indications that it has strong ambitions in the TV, book and merchandising worlds. Not yet, anyway. Another new children's entertainment brand, Finland-based Gigglebug, made its debut as an app to build buzz for the TV show. We'll see more of this from appy start-ups and traditional producers alike.

More trends? Using games for other purposes is interesting at the moment. Nosy Crow's 'Jack and the Beanstalk' takes its cues from gaming in many ways, but only in the service of storytelling. Meanwhile, IF... – developed by a company started by Electronic Arts founder Trip Hawkins – aims to marry *Legend of Zelda*-style production values to deeply researched social and emotional learning theories. Concepts like edutainment and 'serious games' aren't new, but they're getting a new lease of life on tablets.

The last trend that I'm following keenly in 2014, is kids as coders – or at least, kids as potential coders. From this September, computer programming will be part of the school curriculum from a much younger age, at a time when access to tablets – both in the home and at school – is increasing rapidly. There are already a number of apps trying to teach children to code in a fun, engaging way, with more to come.

In the former category, there are apps like 'Hopscotch HD', 'Tynker', 'Hakitzu Elite', 'Move the Turtle', 'Lightbot' and 'Kodable', all trying to teach programming through play. Coming soon, there are more exciting projects: 'ScratchJr' is an app for animation and coding; 'Play-I' is making a pair of robots controlled by companion apps that teach programming skills; 'Kano' is a 'build it yourself' computer based on the Raspberry Pi with its own coding language for kids; and *Hello Ruby* is a book teaching young children first programming concepts through a mix of story and exercises.

There's a burst of innovation around apps and kids and coding in 2014, but something that hasn't been tapped yet is the potential for existing children's brands to slot neatly into that trend. How can we see characters from *SpongeBob SquarePants*, *Angry Birds*, CBeebies, *Skylanders*, *Moshi Monsters*, *The Gruffalo*, *Frozen*, *The Muppets* and/or *The Twits* help children learn to code? I think we'll see more partnerships trying to find out in the near future.

There are lots of challenges in the world of children's apps, particularly around negotiating the pitfalls of in-app purchases and app store marketing. Far too many of those innovative, beautiful, creative etc. apps sink like stones in the unforgiving waters of Apple and Google's stores. And that's a problem. What's more, apps aren't everything: I still think they complement books, TV shows, games and films rather than replace them, whatever 'Kids are all on tablets!!!' zealots might tell you.

But, as a parent and a journalist, I'm more enthusiastic in 2014 than I've ever been about the creative potential of children's apps, and the inventiveness of the community of developers that's making them. I'm sure my own kids would agree. At least, they would if I could peel them away from that potty-mouthed virtual cat...

Screen Media and Children ㉑
A Parent's Perspective
Helen Simmons

For the majority of parents, screen media is now a normal part of everyday life at work and at home. As a parent of a toddler and a six year old, I view screen media as both my friend and foe. I have become increasingly reliant on using it for reward and preoccupation, in order to fulfil day-to-day tasks. It has become my best friend or should I say 'babysitter' during hectic days, so much so that it has nearly replaced my old ally, the television.

The iPad has become the favourite in our house with constant battles of whose turn it is to use it, with the occasional 'iPaddy' thrown in. My toddler loves the various apps that I have downloaded and God forbid when the time comes that he actually realises that more are available to buy! What was originally 'my' iPad has now morphed into 'the children's' iPad, with my fitness apps being replaced with 'Toddler Town' and 'Princess Dress Up'. If only I had an iPad with endless memory! Both children love listening to music we have downloaded on the iPad and on such sites as Vevo and YouTube. Herein lies the problem; this is where screen media turns from my friend to my potential enemy. This, I think, is every parent's nightmare: the internet and children! What once was a reliable babysitter has regressed into a highly unreliable, spotty teenager.

When my children access the internet, I feel myself constantly peeking over their shoulder to see if they are viewing appropriate content, what with the overwhelming threat of Miley Cyrus 'twerking' or Rihanna bearing a naked part of herself in a music video. It doesn't help that my children actually like their music! On a serious note though, I feel that artists like these should take responsibility for the content of their videos and the age of the audience that are viewing. There should at least be a parental guidance or warning before the video can be played. And don't even get me started on the portrayal of women. I will save that for another soapbox!

From a positive perspective, I do think that the internet and screen media have a great deal to offer with regards to children's education. There are so many great educational apps out there, in particular for preschoolers, which can help with the transition to primary school. My daughter's school has invested in an online reading programme, which is excellent as she gains online rewards for each book she reads, that are translated into rewards at school. Programmes like these make you appreciate how beneficial online screen media can be for children, even with all the concerns about internet safety.

My daughter's school holds an internet safety talk annually, and I support this initiative and believe it is something every school should so. We are bombarded daily with stories in the media of cyberbullying and online predators and I have to admit it is something that I worry about – perhaps not as much now, but more in the future when I will have less control over what my children are viewing or whom they are talking too. I am not entirely sure where the solution lies to this problem, but if schools and the government can provide more support on how parents should be tackling these issues then it would surely be for the greater good.

Screen media is here to stay and it will become even more involved in our children's lives in the future. We need to embrace it and all the good things that come with it. I'm sure that there are bound to be exciting developments ahead, and with them, more understanding for parents around their children's safety online, therefore diminishing those fears we all hold in our hearts.

Let Toys Be Toys 22

Alex Lewis Paul

I am a parent of two children: George (nearly five) and Beatrix (nearly one). I got involved campaigning with Let Toys Be Toys (LTBT) at its inception in November 2012, and was asked to speak at the Children's Media Foundation event in November 2013 on LTBT's behalf.

"TV's all rubbish. Read a book."

Preparing to speak to a room of people working in the children's media industry, from the perspective of a sceptical parent, helped me look at why we as a family had tried to avoid TV for our four year old, and whether actually we were making unfounded assumptions about a lack of quality media for children. I realised we had fallen into the trap of thinking that books have intrinsic value while online content and apps are time-wasters; TV is unengaging and passive, and children's magazines are all about cross-selling flimsy merchandise. Taking an objective look at our media consumption habits made me realise we were letting in some enduring classic characters with a leniency they didn't deserve (*Thomas and Friends*, *Bob the Builder*), while missing out on new high quality material (*Katie Morag*, *Octonauts*). We still strongly vet what our four year old watches, and it's always by playing an episode from on-demand TV services, rather than switching on the box, but I'm glad we had the trigger to change.

"Dolls are for girls. Action Man is for boys."

Let Toys be Toys sprang up from a shared belief (and then survey evidence) that the mainstream toy retailers are strongly gender specific in their marketing and aisle or shelf sorting of toys, and that it's clear this trend has become more marked in the past 25 years. We think it limits children's imagination, creates a divide between the sexes which need not be there, and reduces their scope for creativity and learning. Narrow definitions of what a boy or a girl is expected to like to play with, makes play uncomfortable and unenjoyable for a child who doesn't happen to fit into that definition. And while a term like 'tomboy' is not necessarily pejorative for a girl, the reverse for a boy – to be called 'girly' – does seem to be used to indicate undesirable, weak or generally lesser or inferior characteristics.

"What shall we do this weekend, kids?"

As a working parent, I'm conscious that we have limited leisure time that we can spend all together, so we want it to be quality time. Sometimes that is just by making sure it is shared time rather than going off separately to do our own thing, making it leisure and not just doing the chores, or sometimes exploring and learning things together. In particular, as my son is in reception year at school, we've put quite a lot of our weekend into helping him learn his phonics and to read the simple books he gets home from school. I went searching for iPad apps to help with the appropriate level of literacy and numeracy, and was struck by the limited choice even of paid-for apps, in comparison to a wide range of games with purely entertainment value. Perhaps the issue is that what we are prepared to spend our money on in a busy working world is skewed towards buying leisure, while we think that education and development is covered by the professionals in school time? It would explain why, as a society, unconsciously or unthinkingly, we have in recent years allowed toys and games to segregate girls and boys into different interests in a way we wouldn't if it was an educational policy.

"Once upon a time…"

So, in taking a harder look at my assumptions about the value of children's books, I dug out my own vintage 'Read It Yourself' Ladybird books collection, and the other treasured books I had saved since then. I found a fair few fairy tales, but they were the original classics rather than the Disney editions. I was read the Brothers Grimm and Hans Christian Andersen at bedtime (it might explain a lot!) and I don't remember any half term blockbuster animation releases reimagining the storylines. The classic fairy tale is undoubtedly a significant European cultural anchor in which a lot of our fundamental ethics and values, laws and politics, social strata and, of course, gender roles are reflected (and perhaps perpetuated); and though I can't possibly do justice to that idea without learning a lot more about literature, I know it's not as simple as weak princesses, gallant knights, evil stepmothers and faithful servants.

"Go and help your mother with the washing."

For his second birthday, George was given Richard Scarry's *What Do People Do All Day*, a 1970s anthropomorphic canter around basic capitalism and the agricultural, manufacturing and service industries. To my eternal bafflement, it instantly became a firm favourite and is picked out at least once a week at bedtime. I find myself randomly re-gendering the characters as we go along: well, if cats, goats, rabbits and pigs can be coalminers, farmers, tailors, grocers and ocean-going liner captains, making

a few of them women shouldn't be so much of a stretch, surely? But it's subtler than that, as seen in plenty of books and programmes that take a fairly lazy, mum-centric view of whose role it is to keep the domestics running smoothly; for example, while the *Biff, Chip and Kipper* kids have no obvious boy/girl segregation, when it comes to the parents, dad's a bit of a twit and mum always comes up with a sensible solution or rescue. For better representations of equality at home we like *Pingu*, in which dad always does the ironing and usually cooks the dinner; and the Happy Families series of books which cover lots of varied lifestyles and family units (I love *Mrs Plug the Plumber*, and *Mrs Vole the Vet*).

"Daddy's got an important meeting tomorrow."

Similarly, few preschool programmes we know of are much good at representing adult working life to children. In early episodes of *Bob the Builder*, Wendy appears to solely look after the phone and fax in the office, but later she gains a role as project manager, and only in the most recent episodes we've seen can she really be called a builder – see also *Fireman Sam* and *Postman Pat* for women's jobs on the peripheries of vital public services! We debated the new series of *Topsy and Tim* at some length at the CMF event on gender in November 2013. Although I think the back story is that both parents run the family business, it is dad who goes out to the office. Does mum have an accountancy or company secretary qualification and work flexible hours for the business when the children are in school or gone to bed? Possibly, but as far as all the child viewers I've ever eavesdropped on are concerned, what takes place in the waking hours shown in the programme is all that exists, so effectively there's no working woman shown there.

"Wow, look, a Lightning McQueen lunch box! Can I have it, please please?"

I know that merchandising is a fact of life in most of Western society, but it doesn't mean I am going to allow my home to be taken over by it. It must be a loss leader for shops (often seems to be cheaper than plain) perhaps because one piece of character clothing or bedding is never enough and a collection creeps in until, before you know it, you've got an entirely *Peppa Pig* themed wing of your home – sales multiplied! Let Toys Be Toys has heard accounts from some independent toy designers who told us that amongst the big retailers' first considerations in potentially stocking a new line is whether it is seen on TV advertising or a tie-in programme. If no TV time is planned the toy is seen as a risky line to stock, as where would children get the idea how to play with it if there's no story for them to re-enact? Even the archetypal imagination-led toy, LEGO, now has to fill in the gap by creating apps and videos on its website. I can't be alone in finding that sad.

"I would like three stories tonight, mummy. No, four."

Apparently, boys are harder to get interested in reading than girls. Other received wisdom is that boys aren't interested when there is a female central character. Lots of supporters of Let Toys Be Toys badgered us to 'Do books!': so we did. We chose World Book Day in March 2014 to start asking publishers to take the 'For girls' and 'For boys' labels off lots of their lines – sticker books, colouring books, and stories. Amazing support flooded in from huge names in children's literature and poetry, and Children's Laureates past and present. Usborne announced almost immediately that they will not be publishing further gendered titles, "because it is the right thing to do.", and Parragon followed suit soon after. I really hope that this strand of the campaign, with the long overdue spotlight on the increasingly gendered marketing of books, continues to help anyone with a role in helping the next generation navigate through their childhood, to take a more careful look at what messages the toys, books, TV shows and films are presenting them. Tired stereotypes that actually don't reflect modern life? Segregation of subjects that shuts down the growth of interests and skills and children's visibility of potential career paths? Or – the whole wide palette of the real and the imagined world without room to waste on unnecessary genderising?

Anyway, if you'll excuse me, I've got four bedtime stories to read to George, who loves everything about books. We're starting with one about a truly kick-ass princess that gets abducted by aliens.

For All Children
Representations of Gender in Children's Books

Beth Cox

We want children to be readers so that they can explore new worlds and the outer reaches of their imagination, so that they can have somewhere to escape to, and so that they can make sense of the world around them. If we present them with gender stereotypes, then we are denying them that freedom and enjoyment of reading. If the books that children read are reinforcing that they must behave in or appear a certain way (both boys and girls) then we are stunting their development in more ways than one.

The argument is often given that books (and, in fact, all forms of media) are created according to children's like and interests, but rather than reinforcing stereotypical ideas about what girls and boys like, we should be encouraging them to expand their experiences and interests – to think bigger. For example, if your child liked one colour or one type of toy you'd be doing everything you could to get them interested in other things. If some girls really do only like things that are pink and glitter-coated, shouldn't we be encouraging them to widen their horizons? We need to present other options, both for the children that like these things and those that don't. Most importantly, we need to offer choice.

Books should challenge presumptions, not reinforce them. Traditional gender roles are portrayed every day. It is essential that books show something different: that they counter expectations, not just in overt but in subtle ways. It's not a 'tick box' exercise. One book for television show featuring an autonomous girl or a caring boy won't make a difference if every other depiction children see reinforces a gender stereotype. The breaking down of stereotypes needs to happen across the board.

Too often we portray a default setting without really thinking about what we're doing. We need to offer children alternatives to the default stay at home mum; the default male protagonist (especially when it comes to animal characters); the default pink/princess/glitter book cover; the default boisterous boy.

Challenging these defaults can be done both directly and indirectly. The direct challenges seem to happen more often, with an array of books about princesses who don't conform and prefer more typically 'masculine' activities. There are fewer books that overtly depict boys enjoying so-called 'feminine' interests, but they are starting to appear. There are books about aspirational girls, yet less about sensitive boys, and there are books that ask children to question the stereotypes that are so often forced on us, such as *What Are You Playing At?* published by Alanna Books. However, as I've mentioned, it's the indirect messages that we really need to be aware of and challenge. It's important to analyse character depictions to see if boys and girls, men and women, are shown partaking in and enjoying activities that challenge gender stereotypes, even if this is just showing mum driving the car rather than dad (you'd be surprised how rare this is). Are women shown working in, or aspiring to careers in STEM? Are girls shown wearing clothes that are a whole rainbow of colours and in which they can be active? And are they shown with short as well as long hair? Are boys shown enjoying a wide range of fancy dress outfits, including fairy and princess costumes?

In books for older children, is it possible to swap the pronouns of minor characters, so a boss or a thief becomes 'she' instead of 'he'? But a word to content creators: have you unnecessarily used 'female' as a prefix for a paramedic or a firefighter? Question why you have done this. Is it because, by default, you think that these professions are for men and it's noteworthy for a woman to be working in them? Even fairy tales can be adapted. Do all the goats in Billy Goats Gruff have to be male?

Amongst the glut of 'girly' books, we are, thankfully, presented with a number of autonomous female characters; but sensitive, caring, or just non-macho boy characters are few and far between. That's not to say that girls are better off in terms of books. They are constantly being giving mixed messages that imply girls have an innate a fascination with cupcakes and baking, whilst at the same time being bombarded with unrealistic body ideals and encouraged to have a preoccupation with their looks.

The gendering of some particular items can be arbitrary and infuriating. When did butterflies become pink and purple and only of interest to girls? The most common butterfly in this country is the peacock butterfly, known for its vivid red, yellow and black colouring.

There is a strange perception, often promoted by publishers, that all children will read books with male protagonists, but only girls will read books with female protagonists. Why is this, and why is it acceptable? Perhaps it's because books with female protagonists tend to have heavily gendered covers meaning that even if a boy is interested in the contents, he's put off reading it for fear of being teased for choosing a 'girly' book. If books with female characters are marketed just to girls, it says to boys that girls aren't worth reading about. They are given a false sense of entitlement, false notions of masculinity, and miss out the opportunity to empathise with girls. This is key, as reading is how we learn about empathy. Can we really accept that books give a message to boys that girls – and anything that is of interest to girls – are inferior?

> You say you're afraid people will think you're a sissy wimp if they catch you not acting all masculine or something. But why are those the only two possibilities? Why do you have to be either macho or a sissy? Why can't you just be whoever you are?
> *Parrotfish*, Ellen Wittlinger

Gender is not binary, it is a spectrum, and creating and marketing products to the extremes of the spectrum means that the children in the middle are left out, and confused about where they fit in.

> There aren't only two genders, and not all kids are sure of their gender identity, and the question ,"Is this a girl book or a boy book?" shuts those kids out and makes them invisible, when quite frankly, they've got more than enough sh*t to deal with already.
> Tom Pollock, Author
> http://tompollock.com/2013/03/07/always-should-be-something-you-really-love/

Every time we distinguish between boys and girls, we tell children that there is a difference, thereby promoting inequality.

> Those involved in producing and purchasing books for children owe it to them to recognise and value differences between genders, but at the same time hold equal aspirations for them. Authors, illustrators, publishers, editors, booksellers and book buyers need to be vigilant about challenging restrictive assumptions about gender roles and preferences.
> Lizzie Poulton and Irene Picton
> 'Gendered Marketing in Children's Books' *Write4Children*, Vol. IV, Issue II, June 2013

One of the main reasons that things are this way is because of pressure from accounts or outside agencies. We've got ourselves into a trap where we think that things have to be gendered in order to sell, and therefore producing something that is not defined by gender is seen as more risky.

Publishers involved with licensing and branding seem to think that if someone is interested in buying the license for a character wants to create gendered products to tie in to a book or TV programme then they can't say no. I'd argue that, if, as a publisher, someone wants to buy your product, you're in a powerful position to refuse such terms: to impose a condition that the product can't be gendered. If it's a popular product, it will sell anyway. Big companies are more likely to be able to afford to take that so-called 'risk', yet it's often the small independent companies who are the ones who stand up to such things and try to forge a better path, and who therefore take risks. They aren't guaranteed the same levels of sales as a big corporation, but they put their businesses on the line on a regular basis because their ethics come first and they are trying to make a difference.

Companies obviously need to stay in business and make money, but children are *our* business, all our business, and the messages that we are giving them should be of far greater concern than the bottom line.

Self-publishing and the Children's Book Market 24
Rob Keeley

You may have heard of self-publishing, but what does this actually mean?

Within the traditional literary world the term 'self-publishing' still is occasionally met with a raised eyebrow. With readers who buy or borrow books, including for their children, a lot of myths can still endure. "Self-publishing? So the author's paid for the book to be published? Can't be much good then." "They can't hope to sell many. Maybe a few copies to family, or friends down the pub..." "They just churn them out. They're badly written. Who can produce three books in three years? No wonder they've never been accepted."

So, self-publishing - the last refuge of the desperate author?

Wrong.

What if I were to tell you that self-publishing is a serious creative activity, has the potential to be a successful business venture and is a phenomenon that the wider publishing world can no longer ignore? And what if I went on to say that self-published children's books have emerged as a whole new medium, introducing young people to brand new characters and stories and fictional worlds? That self-publishing represents a completely new area of specialism within the children's media landscape? Read on...

So what is self-publishing?

Self-publishing essentially means that the author takes primary control of the production, the publishing, and sometimes the marketing of their own book. These processes will be funded by the author, but this is rewarded with a far higher level of creative input than the traditional, commercially-published author usually enjoys. Self-publishing can also be rewarded with a far greater percentage for the author in terms of royalties than with traditional publishing – though the author has to sell enough copies to recoup their initial outlay!

It's no longer simply a matter of producing copies for family and friends. Many publishing companies now offer a self-publishing service that works very much like the traditional publishing process, with

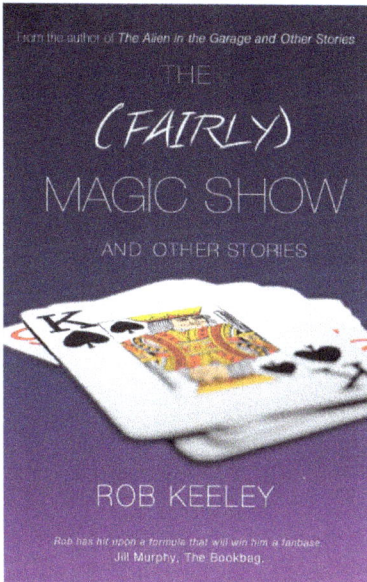

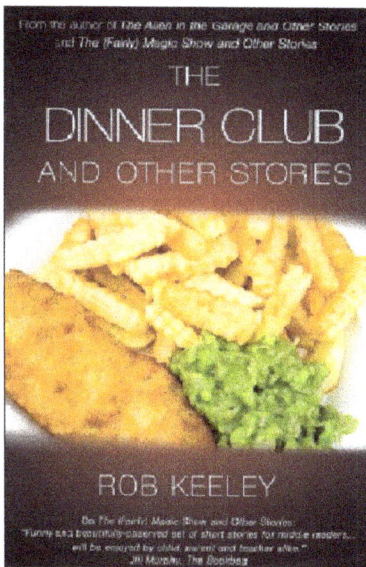

editorial, proofreading and marketing services similar to those a commercially-published author receives. The difference being, of course, that the self-published author is paying! But the self-published author is also in a particularly strong position to determine how the finished book will look and how it will be marketed, as well as what it will contain. If you want a spooky door on the cover of your first book for children (as I did), or want the book to be printed on cream-coloured paper (as I did), or want review copies to be sent to publications of your choice (as I did), then this is exactly what happens. A good self-publishing company will advise, and occasionally put its foot down if it feels something isn't right, but essentially the author is in charge of their own project. For an increasing number of authors, self-publishing offers hope of publication where traditional publishers simply could not accommodate their work.

But if a book for children is good, why don't traditional publishers take it?

Like any commercial company, a traditional publisher is primarily concerned with what it thinks it can sell. The children's book market is infamously competitive. In the economic conditions of recent years, traditional publishers want to make sure that books they take on will sell in their thousands, if not millions. Anything that seems not to fit into 'our current list' (to quote a popular phrase from rejection letters) tends to be a risk a commercial publisher will not take. Much of the time this is down to the judgment of the individual editor. The process is a constant source of frustration to the author who knows their idea is good.

These conditions leave relatively little room for the unusual or experimental, or indeed sometimes even for the overly traditional children's book. Anything that seems too way-out, or too old-fashioned, or not to offer potential for a series or follow-ups, may fall foul of traditional publishers' requirements, despite the fact that in all these cases there will be children, parents and teachers out there who would enjoy the book.

Nor is it true to say that self-publishing equals lesser quality. A point often forgotten is that a discerning self-publishing company may apply a quality threshold before it will agree to publish a book. Like the traditional publisher, it wants to protect its brand, and will only accept a book that seems to have sales potential. But unlike the traditional publisher, it does not commit its own money in doing so. So promising authors now have a way to reach readers without finding themselves stifled by market forces.

Ultimately, the child reading a book, or having it read to them, doesn't care how the book was published. They just want it to be good. And self-publishing means the young reader will receive opportunities for adventure, or laughter, or self-discovery that they would otherwise never have encountered.

How self-publishing can succeed

I entered the world of self-publishing in 2011, having had it recommended to me by a friend. I'd had one or two 'near misses' with traditional publishers, going back nearly a decade, but my short stories and novels for children ultimately hadn't fitted into any 'current list'. Despite received wisdom about brands and target groups and the need to pitch at very specific audiences, I knew there was still a market for my short story collection, *The Alien in the Garage and Other Stories*, which offered stories for both girls and boys on a variety of themes. Surely there were still 'story times' and private reading sessions? Surely shorter fiction was a good way to coax the eight to twelve year old reader into longer texts? And why shouldn't a book offer something for everyone? I believed in my ideas and in my understanding of the modern young audience. Rather than writing to be published, I was writing simply to be read.

Three years later, I've had two more children's short story collections self-published and I have a children's novel ready to follow. My self-published books are being used in schools and children's libraries and have been entered for two literary prizes. I've visited two literary/arts festivals, have held successful signings and now write for *Self Publishing Magazine*. My success story, if it can be called that, is not an isolated one, and the growing visibility of self-published authors within the literary world means that self-publishing is no longer a medium that can be ignored.

So what does this mean for those of us working in the wider world of children's media?

It can be argued that self-published books for children represent a whole new medium, and one which offers a great source of creative content when so little funding is now available for quality children's media generally. Self-published children's books have entered the marketplace in hardback, paperback and eBook form, the latter being of great value at a time when tablet and mobile platforms are in constant need of fresh and innovative content. Self-published authors have to recognise the impact of digital media on the traditional publishing world, and must be as ready to produce books for an e-reader as they are for printed format. They also have to be ready to produce tie-in material across a variety of media, whether this means downloadable content from their own websites or using blogs or podcasts to take their stories and characters further. The creative and commercial opportunities for those who work in these media are obvious.

Like any artist, the self-published author has to know their audience. They need a specialist understanding of writing for children, and what young people will find funny, or exciting, or intriguing. They have to know what works in children's fiction and what doesn't, and at what stage of emotional development their readers are. It can't be any coincidence that a number of teachers, parents and grandparents have turned to self-publishing!

Visits to schools, libraries and festivals – as well as my past role as a volunteer classroom assistant – have given me the opportunity to meet the audience for my books. And of course, what we learn at such meetings feeds back into our future work. The relatively speedy access that self-publishing provides to the publishing queue – though it should be understood that there is still a queue, in which a book is likely to stand for at least six months – offers potential for contemporary subjects to be dealt with in book form while they are still topical.

For what audience is the modern children's author writing?

Contemporary writing for children has to take traditional children's writing techniques and concepts and adapt them for a modern young audience. This means keeping stories engaging, exciting, humorous and insightful, while avoiding any material unsuitable for a particular age group and its stage of development. At the same time, stories should be set in a recognisable modern world where children have smartphones, are not all from nuclear families and come from a range of social and cultural backgrounds. If the setting for a story is pure fantasy, then it should have enough recognisable grounding in our own world for children to be able to relate to it, or to resolve their own issues in allegorical form. Escapism is only valid if we have somewhere to return to.

And how does this tie in with the wider media?

With homegrown television and film production for children now increasingly constricted, literature has the opportunity to return to fill the gap. Visual content imported from other countries should be counterbalanced by published stories that reflect the lives, aspirations and concerns of a modern young UK audience. In other words, if children in the UK can no longer watch programmes or movies with characters like themselves, they can at least read about them. I was fortunate enough to grow up in the '80s and early '90s when such programming was plentiful, and I believe I learned as much from children's television of that period as from books of the same era, when it came to devising children's stories of my own.

At the same time as preserving a literary tradition, books for children have to work with newer media such as e-publishing and podcasts to adapt themselves to the ever changing technological tastes of the new generation. Self-published authors have the advantage of bringing their work directly to readers without first having to overcome the hurdle of preconceived ideas on what children should be reading – thereby testing the market for their own books.

The traditional commercial publishing world now has an opportunity to use self-publishing as a talent pool to fill gaps in the existing market. This is already beginning to happen, with self-publishing companies using subscriber online databases to advertise the availability of literary, film or television rights to commercial publishers and the wider media. The self-published author of today could produce the bestselling children's novel or movie success or TV hit of tomorrow. And if children like it, and parents like it, and teachers like it, and a work is a success, then surely everyone is happy? The readers of my books certainly seem to be.

FAREWELL

Richard Briers 1934-2013
Torin Douglas

One Sunday afternoon in April this year, the Criterion Theatre in Piccadilly Circus was full to the brim with actors, writers, directors, producers – and others with no connection at all to the worlds of TV and theatre, other than friendship. They were there to celebrate the life and work of one of Britain's best loved actors and entertainers, Richard Briers.

When the lights in the theatre went down, they were treated to a three-minute video clip – not from *The Good Life* or *Monarch of the Glen* or *The Norman Conquests* or *Ever Decreasing Circles* or *Twelfth Night* or *Hamlet* or *Frankenstein* or any of the other films and TV series Richard was famous for – but from the cartoon series, *Roobarb*.

Never can so many distinguished actors and producers have laughed so hard at the antics of a yellow cartoon dog and purple cat, aided – of course – by Richard's sublime voiceover.

It was a surreal and inspired opening to an hour long appreciation of the work of Richard Briers, but it was also a reminder of the contribution he made to productions for children, as well as adults, on television, film and the stage.

The first series of *Roobarb* episodes (30 x 5 mins) was broadcast in 1974 on BBC One, just before the early evening news, and with its wobbly animation and manic characters it acquired cult status among adults as well as being loved by children. 30 years later, in 2005, a new series was made – *Roobarb & Custard Too* – with Richard giving voice to the characters as well as acting as narrator.

The success *of Roobarb* led to more voiceover work. In 1975, Richard was the narrator for an animated version of *Noddy* and in 1978 he was the voice of Fiver, one of the central characters in the animated film version of *Watership Down*. Twenty years later, when a fifteen part TV series was made, he played a new character, Captain Broom.

The Wind in the Willows was a natural vehicle for Richard's talents. In 1991, he played Ratty on the stage in Nicholas Hytner's memorable National Theatre production, written by Alan Bennett. He also voiced the character in several adaptations on radio and TV, including *The Adventures of Toad* and *The Adventures of Mole.*

Always in demand as a voiceover artist, Richard even played *Bob the Builder*'s dad, Robert – and one of his last roles was as the voice of the Mouse, opposite Alan Bennett's Mole, in a half-hour animated film, *The Mouse and the Mole* at Christmas time.

Richard was loved by viewers and listeners of all generations; they felt they knew him personally, because of his particular presence on their screens. But those who were fortunate to know him in person loved him even more, as testified by the tributes from his colleagues and his neighbours in Chiswick, many of whom were invited to the Criterion celebration of his life.

Sir Kenneth Branagh, who was instrumental in Richard's move from popular comedy parts on television to major Shakespearean roles on film and the stage, said, "He was a national treasure, a great actor and a wonderful man. He was greatly loved and he will be deeply missed."

Dame Penelope Keith, one of his co-stars in *The Good Life*, said, "I look back with enormous affection and love for Dickie. He was the most talented of actors, always self-deprecating. He was courteous and he would speak to the crew – which was not always that common. It was the most enjoyable time: when I think of *The Good Life*, I smile."

Bob Godfrey 1921-2013
Tony Collingwood

Bob Godfrey passed away last year, aged 91. He was, without a doubt, the best loved animation director of his generation. A bombastic, hilarious, shy, talented man who cared deeply about the animation industry and, more importantly, about the people in it – all of whom are saddened by his passing.

Though born in Australia, his parents moved to England in the 1920s, whilst Bob was still very young. Bob's career was long and fruitful, directing a series of wonderful short films, including *Henry 9 'til 5*, *Kama Sutra Rides Again*, and the Oscar winning *Great*, amongst many others.

His kids' shows are still well remembered, especially *Roobarb*, *Noah & Nelly* and *Henry's Cat*. (Bob once told me that he voiced *Henry's Cat* himself as it was cheaper than hiring an actor!)

However, I would argue that his greatest legacy must be the legions of animators and artists who have Bob to thank for their start in the business. The starting point for many of us, myself included, was a television programme first broadcast in 1974, called *The Do-It-Yourself Film Animation Show*, a series presented by Bob, which not only showcased the work of top-flight practitioners like Richard Williams and Terry Gilliam but also revealed how amazingly raw and simple animation could be. He showed that you didn't have to be able to draw like a Disney animator to have fun in the medium. The biggest revelation being that *anyone* could do it! And from that point on, many of us did...

Throughout his career he continually visited art colleges and attended festivals – always engaging with those starting out in the industry. We fed off Bob's anarchy and enthusiasm – anything was possible.

So many student animators passed through his thin, three-storey studio in Neal Street during the '70s and '80s. I remember coming down from Liverpool Art College to work for him as a runner – my first paid job – and he allowed me to sleep under a light box in the studio for a fortnight!

So, on behalf of many generations of animators, I'd just like to say "Thanks, Bob!" for drawing so many of us into this crazy, wonderful business.

We miss you.

Jocelyn Hay 1927-2014

Colin Browne

Described by the broadcasting critic, Gillian Reynolds, as "possibly the best lobbyist in the whole UK," Jocelyn Hay's initial exposure to broadcasting came in somewhat unlikely circumstances. She was a very youthful contributor to British Forces Broadcasting in Trieste, where her father was stationed immediately after the Second World War. Nearly forty years years later, she was already a significant figure in the media world when, in 1983, through a successful campaign against plans to turn BBC Radio 4 into an all news and current affairs network, she founded the Voice of the Listener. A freelance broadcaster and a Fellow of the Institute of Public Relations she was also, from 1973 to 1978, Head of Press and Public Relations at the Girl Guide Commonwealth Headquarters. In addition she continued to direct the training agency, London Media Workshops, which specialised in writing, directing and producing radio, television and video programmes, until 1994.

It is, however, her work for the Voice of the Listener and Viewer (VLV) – the 'Viewer' was added in 1993 – for which she will be best remembered. VLV was born out of Jocelyn's firm belief that, "We put the cause of the listener and viewer first" and her fierce advocacy of the role of public service broadcasting in civil society.

When I joined the BBC in 1994, there were plenty in the Corporation who bore the scars of Jocelyn's lobbying. Some queried what a woman from outside the mainstream of the industry really knew about broadcasting and felt that it was best that such matters were left to the professionals; in short, what right had the 'ordinary' viewer or listener to have a say in such issues? But there was nothing ordinary about Jocelyn and many in the BBC came to recognise that her commitment to quality in television and radio was a huge asset to all who really cared – as she did – about the future of British broadcasting and the quality of the national debate.

Under Jocelyn's leadership, VLV, in the words of the academic and media commentator, Roy Greenslade, "emerged as the most important champion of television and radio consumers by consistently pressing for the retention and extension of high quality public service broadcasting.' Another media executive turned academic, Stewart Purvis, noted the importance of Jocelyn's personal contribution:

When Jocelyn Hay calls you tend to listen. It is partly the voice. I wasn't surprised to discover that she was once a senior official in the Girl Guides. And it is partly respect for the woman who is a kind of Florence Nightingale of public service broadcasting, supporting the hard-worked troops on the front line while looking ahead to even more complicated issues.

In considering such issues she tirelessly advocated the cause of listeners and viewers at local meeting places and in rooms accessed from the corridors of power. She was particularly proud of the way that VLV advanced the recognition of citizen and consumer interests in broadcasting in the UK, European and international arenas. These included membership of OFTEL's Consumer Advisory Panel, the Government Stakeholder Group on Digital Television, the Steering Group of the European Information Society Forum and the Council of the European Institute for the Media.

The quality – and availability – of children's programming was always close to her heart. Under her leadership, and working closely with a number of interested groups – including the British Action for Children's Television (BACTV) – the VLV established, in 1995, the first of a regular series of conferences on children's programming, bringing together producers, researchers, policy makers, educators and students. VLV's Special Group for Children's Broadcasting kept up the pressure on the public service broadcasters – for example, receiving, in 1996, an assurance from the then BBC Chairman that a commitment to children's programming would be included in the revised statement of BBC's Pledges to its Audiences (having been omitted from the first version).

Jocelyn never defended the status quo for its own sake. While recognising the substantial and significant demand for traditional channels, she wrote, in 2006, that, in the future, "we'll be watching television in many different and totally new ways, through our computers in the office, through mobile phones, in all sorts of ways." She tirelessly advocated the cause of consumers in the many official and unofficial fora in which she was invited to participate, and not just in the UK. She was the first consumer representative to be invited to give oral evidence to a Hearing of the Council of Europe and she was the Founder President of the European Alliance of Listeners and Viewers' Associations (EURALVA) from 1995-2007.

Having been appointed an MBE in 1999, she was made a CBE in 2005 for her work with VLV. She was awarded the Elizabeth R Award for an Exceptional Contribution to Public Service Broadcasting by the Commonwealth Broadcasting Association in 1999 and in 2007 was presented with a European Women of Achievement Award by the European Union of Women.

Since Jocelyn's death, I have been struck by the range of people and organisations who have spoken about her – from the worlds of broadcasting and the media, and, more generally, consumer and civil society groups, academia, politicians and the EU. All have been inspired in one way or another by Jocelyn, as have I.

Lord Hall, Director General of the BBC, said:

> Jocelyn Hay had a huge impact on broadcasting in this country. She never stopped campaigning for better quality programmes and for all broadcasters to put their audiences first. She always believed it was every broadcaster's duty to make engaging programmes that captured the public's imagination. She will be much missed.

The BBC's Chairman, Lord Patten, wrote:

> Jocelyn was an absolutely indomitable campaigner for better quality across TV and radio, and a staunch advocate of public service broadcasting and all it stands for. She was an inspiration to many over the 30 years of campaigning, creating the VLV and turning it into the powerful force for good that it is today.

Jon Snow called her an "exceptional woman... she was so good for us all whichever side of the camera or microphone we lived'; and Melvyn Bragg spoke of losing "somebody important" in the field of broadcasting.

In 1993, Jocelyn wrote, "Ten years ago the threats were vague and distant. Now they are real: in some cases overwhelming. We must redouble our efforts if the quality and richness of British broadcasting is to be maintained."

As we face another period of intense media policy making, twenty years on from that statement, the VLV will be determined to ensure that the principles espoused by Jocelyn are maintained.

Jimmy T. Murakami 1933-2014
Michael Algar

Jimmy Murakami, who died after a brief illness aged 80, was a Japanese-American animation director. He is widely considered as a founding father of the Irish animation industry, having lived and worked in Ireland since 1970.

Born Teruaki Murakami in San Jose to Japanese parents, he was interned, aged eight, with his family when the US entered the Second World War. Although US citizens, Jimmy's family (along with thousands of others of Japanese origin) was considered a threat to national security. Living in the internment camp for five years at Tule Lake – a desert wasteland in northern California – gave Jimmy a lifelong dislike of men in uniforms giving orders. Obliged to choose a western name, he chose Jimmy after the actor Jimmy Stewart. Unwittingly, his brother Junichi chose James! So they went through their later film careers as Jimmy T. Murakami and James J. Murakami.

Following his release in 1946, he completed schooling and was interested in becoming a brain surgeon. However, after six months of medical college he won a three year scholarship to study art and animation at the Chouinard Art Institute (later part of CalArts). There's no doubt that he would have applied just as much energy and enthusiasm to medicine as he subsequently did to painting and filmmaking.

In 1956 he was headhunted from college by UPA Burbank Studio to work, and then moved to Pintoff Studio in New York where he animated *The Violinist*, an Oscar-nominated short. After an unhappy year at Toei Animation in Tokyo, in 1960 he moved to London as a producer and director at TV Cartoons. There he directed *The Insects* (BAFTA nominated) and *Charley* (Venice Gold Lion winner) amongst other short films.

Returning to Los Angeles in 1965, with Fred Wolf he established Murakami Wolf as a studio for theatrical shorts, television specials, documentary films and commercials. He won the Annecy Grand Prix for *Breath*, produced *The Magic Pear Tree* (Oscar nominated), *And Of Course You* (Golden Eagle award), *The Good Friend* (inaugural AFI grant) and many other films.

In 1970 Jimmy came to Dublin as Associate Producer and aerial sequence director on *Von Richthofen and Brown*, a First World War live-action feature film. He married Ethna McInerney and remained in Ireland, establishing Quateru Film to produce award winning live-action and animation commercials. He returned to LA in 1980 to direct another live-action feature *Battle Beyond the Stars* (on which he gave James Cameron his first job as art director). Jimmy always regarded himself as a filmmaker rather than solely an animator.

In 1982 he was asked to direct *The Snowman*, from the Raymond Briggs book, at TVC in London. He turned down the role as director in favour of being supervising director. It went on to become one of the best-loved animated films, winning a BAFTA award and an Oscar nomination. In 1986 at TVC he adapted and directed another Raymond Briggs book, *When the Wind Blows*, which won the Feature Grand Prix at Annecy Animation Festival in 1987. Made on a low budget, *When the Wind Blows* tells the story of an old couple trying to cope with an imminent nuclear war. It used innovative techniques to combine miniature model sets with hand-drawn animation and featured the voices of John Mills and Peggy Ashcroft.

In 1989 he helped Fred Wolf to establish Murakami Wolf in Dublin (often referred to as MWD) to produce *Teenage Mutant Ninja Turtles*, the long-running TV series. The studio had a staff of over 100 artists. Many of them were art school graduates who were trained in animation at the studio. Former MWD people are now working at Disney, DreamWorks and other studios around the world.

Jimmy continued to work in Dublin and overseas, directing *The Storykeepers* hit TV series in Dublin in 1995; *Inspector Mouse* in Paris in 1997; and *Oi Get Off Our Train* in London in 1998. He directed another animated feature in London (in 2000) – *Christmas Carol: The Movie* (with Kate Winslet performing and singing, and other voices including Michael Gambon, Nicolas Cage, Simon Callow and Jane Horrocks) – and, in 2005, a music video with Kate Bush, *King of the Mountain*.

In 2010, Jimmy was the subject of a feature documentary, *Jimmy Murakami – Non Alien*, in which he revisited the internment camp at Tule Lake.

Throughout all his years in Dublin, he tutored, mentored and lectured young aspiring animators. The current healthy animation sector in Ireland is due in no small measure to his continuous involvement. He was a regular guest lecturer at IADT Dun Laoghaire and the Irish School of Animation in Ballyfermot. In recognition of his contribution to the world of animation, Dundee University awarded him an honorary doctorate in 2006. In March 2013, Dingle International Film Festival inaugurated the annual Murakami Award in his honour.

Last year he celebrated his 80th birthday developing *The Morning of a Hundred Suns*, a feature film based on his reaction to the Hiroshima bomb. He had also returned to his original love of painting – figurative and landscape – working in oils and watercolours. At the time of his death he had commissions for several new works.

A regular invited guest at film festivals around the world, Jimmy invariably held audiences spellbound with stories and reminiscences. His life experiences were extensive and enriching, and he delighted in sharing his insights. The work he created over the years is a portfolio of tasteful, socially aware, ethical films.

Jimmy is survived by his wife Ethna, daughters Deirdre and Claire, and four grandchildren Keelin, Rory, Finn and Tara.

BBC Television Centre
Centre of Excellence
Richard Marson

Richard Marson spent the best part of twenty years working at Television Centre, many of them in the Children's Department. He was editor of Blue Peter *for four years. In 2011, he produced and directed a 90-minute documentary about the place,* Tales of Television Centre. *Here, he looks back at the long history of children's programmes at this most iconic of buildings.*

The winter of 1963 was the coldest in living memory. The chill winds and arctic temperatures must have seemed an entirely appropriate climate for the staff at BBC Children's, who had just discovered that the department was to be dismantled and most of them (if they were lucky) packed off to work in other areas in the Corporation.

Although much in the world of television has changed beyond recognition over the past 50 years, the politics and machinations at the top of the game have remained a constant, and it was these that inspired this sudden and brutal dissolution. The man wielding the axe was the Controller of BBC One, Stuart Hood, fed up with what he perceived to be the inadequacies of the department and its beleaguered head, Owen Reed. Hood's decision was to merge Children's with another 'ghetto' department (Women's Programmes), to form the hybrid 'Family Programmes'. In this new model, only a skeleton of the original output of the Children's Department survived.

The nucleus of remaining staff may have been bemused and bitter, but they were also vocational and determined and, over the next few years, fought the logic of the merger with a steady surge of creativity and imagination. It was during this period that *Blue Peter* emerged from the doldrums to become a powerhouse. Another perennial, *Play School*, arrived with the start of BBC Two in 1964. Stellar storytelling strand, *Jackanory*, followed the year after. Finally, BBC senior management recognised the error of judgement that had been made and, in 1967, the Children's Department was reborn. Significantly, this coincided with a move from offices based in Kensington House (in nearby Shepherd's Bush), to the brutalist heights of the East Tower of Television Centre.

The East Tower was far from being the height of luxury but its position, perched on the periphery of the Centre, did offer some advantages, as long-serving producer/director Jeremy Swan recalls:

> From my office you could see right down to the main entrance where guests would enter the building. When I was casting, I used to keep a pair of binoculars handy and take a look at the actors walking up the road to see me. If I didn't like the look of them, I'd shout out to my secretary, "No coffee for this one, Lesley!"

Then-researcher and future Head of Department, Anna Home, remembers the excitement of the move to the new HQ:

> It felt like entering the grown-up world. Even in the impractical, asbestos-laden East Tower meant being where the action was. Children's was a constant presence around the place with regular series in the studios. It meant we always had a profile: important to a department that could easily have become 'out of sight and out of mind'. It also meant relatively easy access to the big bosses on the sixth floor, and the chance of casual meetings in the lifts, the corridors and even the loo, giving you a chance to argue your case or pitch your project.

Under the inspired leadership of Monica Sims and Edward Barnes (Sims's deputy and then successor), throughout the 1970s the ambition and scale of the department steadily increased and much of this was fuelled and reinforced by their presence at Television Centre. New opportunities were explored and new technology harnessed. When *Blue Peter* moved to colour in 1970, it made a permanent move to the Centre and, not content with filling a rotation of the biggest and best studios (for which there was inevitably fierce competition) with everything from marching bands to double-decker buses, it soon began to press other areas of the building into service too, staging anything from pantomime-horse races to fire bucket chains in the inner circle (known to staff as 'the doughnut'); demonstrating vehicles and gadgets in the two ring roads, on the roof spaces and – irritatingly for the high-ups who didn't wish to be prevented from using it – from the 'horseshoe' car park at the front of the building. Seeking permission to land a helicopter here, editor Biddy Baxter was admonished, "You're turning this into a place of entertainment!"

Every Christmas, *Blue Peter* welcomed an excited crowd of lantern holding, carol singing children as they processed 'up the hill' (actually the service road leading to the multi-storey car park) and into the studio. Perhaps most famously, there was the *Blue Peter* garden, niftily converted from a little piece of wasteland just outside the restaurant block in 1974 and used frequently afterwards, as an integral part of the show, for over 30 years. When the BBC announced their decision to abandon Television Centre, one of the first questions journalists asked was, "What will happen to the *Blue Peter* garden?" This hadn't been anticipated and I received frantic calls in the *Blue Peter* office to help devise some kind of response. In the event, a small section of the garden was transplanted to Salford's MediaCity.

Another stalwart children's classic, *Record Breakers*, was actually a *Blue Peter* spin-off and, like its parent programme, frequently used the scale and facilities of the Centre to mount studio spectaculars, culminating in the oft-repeated 1977 tap dancing stunt around the 'doughnut'. It has been copied since but nothing could replicate the impact of the original.

Thanks to a pioneering partnership with news, Edward Barnes was empowered to devise the trailblazing *John Craven's Newsround*, which arrived, on a trial basis, in 1972. From this tentative, experimental start, it eventually became a cornerstone of the output. But it was only possible because of Television Centre. Similarly, the whole dynasty of hugely successful and influential live Saturday morning output all started when a BBC executive had a dig at Barnes: "You're doing fairly well during the week," he commented, "but your performance at the weekends is pretty hopeless." Barnes was incensed. "It's not bloody surprising," he fumed, "when there's only the money to show a lot of dog-eared repeats…" Back came the response: "Find me the right idea and I'll find you the money…"

It was a challenge which no self-respecting programme maker could resist and producer Rosemary Gill came up with the answer – a virtually unrehearsed live Saturday morning programme called *Multi-Coloured Swap Shop*. Central to the genius of the premise was, again, that it used to the max the facilities and opportunities presented by transmitting from Television Centre. Presenter Noel Edmonds could (and did) get up from behind his desk and take a wander into previously unseen fire lanes and behind the scenes areas. The technicians had a fit but soon got over the heresy of the approach. Viewers loved it when Noel 'dropped in' to the studio next door, to hobnob with the cast of *Dad's Army* or *It Ain't Half Hot Mum* or whatever was happening close by. It added to the sense of 'live' and also to the charming feeling there was a kind of 'family' of stars for whom the Centre was home.

This might seem a little on the sentimental side but it is certainly true that many VIPs who might never otherwise have been persuaded to appear on children's TV, did so simply because it was under the same roof as the top news and current affairs programmes and the big entertainment and comedy shows. Another Saturday morning presenter, Sarah Greene, remembers: "One Friday, I noticed that French and Saunders were rehearsing in another studio. We asked them if they'd like to pop in and they did. It was that simple and that effective."

The same principle enlivened children's presentation when they started to transmit 'in-vision continuity' from the 'broom cupboard' (actually a small presentation studio) in 1985, initially presented by a callow young man called Phillip Schofield. Noteworthy guests could and did make the detour to the fourth floor to take part. These short moments between programmes eventually became part of the identity of CBBC and the template for what has grown into the 'front of house' approach for today's CBBC channel.

Children's drama and entertainment, which, following Hood's dissolution, had been absorbed by the adult departments, gradually made a return until they were once again a steady element in the schedules. There were long-running comedies like *Rentaghost* and *Uncle Jack* and lavish serials like *The Box of Delights*, *Tom's Midnight Garden* and *The Chronicles of Narnia*. For its first few years, *Grange Hill* was based at Television Centre and, as Anna Home vividly recalls, "At times there would be hordes of *Grange Hill* kids storming through main reception!"

Other genres were reactivated, too – game shows, music programmes, topical debates, and a smorgasbord of imaginative preschool offerings – until, by the 1980s, the department was delivering a staggeringly rich mix of content across every genre: effectively its own miniature television service, all operating from Television Centre.

Children's programme have always worked with restricted budgets but in the halcyon years before Director General John Birt unleashed his take-no-prisoners, free market economy within the Corporation, many major aspects of a programme's budget were centrally allocated – from staffing and studios to filming and craft facilities. This meant that children's programmes had access to the same world class resources as the primetime shows. Because the building housed such a rich diversity of talent and experience, there was always someone to turn to for help or advice to help solve the myriad of production problems. It was also possible to 'rob Peter to pay Paul'. Presenter Johnny Ball remembers walking around the 'inner ring road' where surplus scenery was often stored, spotting pieces which he could then ask his producer to 'borrow' for re-use on their ingenious *Think* series – at minimal cost. A vast collection of 'small props' housed in the basement under the design building could be plundered with no impact on the programme's 'above the line' budget; likewise, the rails of stock costumes and wigs and the well-stocked libraries of music, books and journals.

On both sides of the screen, children's programmes were invariably a potent springboard for talent. It is surely one of the reasons why so many 'movers and shakers' of the industry seemed to feel the loss of the Centre so keenly. This was the place where so many of them had cut their teeth. Another former CBBC boss, Anne Gilchrist, looks back:

> The other evening I was looking up a song by Gary Barlow on YouTube (don't ask) and it reminded me of a short sketch I directed on *The Ant & Dec Show* way back when. There it was, endlessly available to a new generation of uninitiated and presumably bemused viewers. I chuckled, more at the memory of making it, than at its intrinsic comic value as I'm not sure it has stood the test of time. But it reminded me of the enormous pride we used to take, as producers, in finding new talent and giving them a gig. As we were so often dealing with inexperienced talent, the job of producing actually meant that - working really hard to help bring out the best in them. There was no formula, each was an individual with differing strengths and weaknesses, but all, to my mind, had a genuine X factor. An astoundingly high percentage of them have gone on to become central figures in the output of our mainstream channels – some of them acknowledging their roots in children's TV, others preferring to sweep those years under the carpet.

> Presenters were taught how to deliver a script on autocue, to manage live TV, to work within a team, to interview, to research, to time their speech up to important junctions, to dress up in costumes they wouldn't necessarily have chosen for themselves, to experiment with ideas, to communicate with a young audience without talking down to them, and to help kids relax, laugh, and benefit from 'soft learning' long after the school gates had clanged shut. There was a potent concoction of fun mixed with danger that often exploded into originality and it was a fabulous privilege to be on the studio floor or in the gallery witnessing it. On every show you would fight to get the very best and most engaged crews who, once 'discovered' by Children's, were immediately lured away to work on more 'important', high-profile adult shows. We were continually trying to wring every ounce of value out of our budgets and the most talented craftsmen and women who got stuck in to help invariably contributed way beyond their pay grade.

"I loved my time at TVC," Gilchrist concludes, "fighting to be outrageous, pushing for inventiveness and creativity and being surrounded by people who were far more talented than me and who, on a good day, could possibly create a few unsurpassable golden childhood memories for an audience who took no prisoners."

Over the years, there were frequent accusations that the Children's Department was too 'London-centric', despite productions regularly based in Bristol, Glasgow, Birmingham and Newcastle – and an entire satellite children's department in Manchester. "Absolutely untrue," insists Biddy Baxter: "On *Blue Peter* we had an average weekly postbag of 7,000 letters from viewers. There were inevitably criticisms, but never, ever that we were focused on London. And we weren't 'London-centric'. Much of the content of each programme stemmed from suggestions sent in by children from every corner of the UK."

"We tried not to be London-centric," agrees Anna Home, "reflecting the whole UK through our content and working with the various active children's hubs outside London in different places at different times. Remember Liverpool?" (Liverpool was, briefly, another of the 'regional hubs' called upon to produce children's programmes for the BBC).

Anna's predecessor, Edward Barnes, argues that because these 'hubs' were created for logistical and political rather than programme-making reasons, this inevitably impaired their effectiveness: "It immediately produced a 'one bloke two Guv'nors' situation," he explains. "In Manchester, for example, the producers were employed using Children's Programmes money but they were not part of the Children's Programmes ethos. This was not a template for the pursuit of excellence and a lot of programmes were of a 'ho hum' standard. There were, of course, exceptions. But there is a reason why talent migrates to London. It's the capital city, after all. It's where many of the best creative people want to be."

Whatever the efforts made to reflect diversity in the output, mounting political pressure on the BBC meant that a major shift in their production base was inevitable. The first rumours that Children's was to be relocated to Salford surfaced in 2003 and were whispered throughout the corridors and stairways of East Tower; but the actual move – a colossally complex and expensive operation – only took place in 2011. The man who led that move is the current Director of BBC Children's, Joe Godwin. He took with him his own happy memories of Television Centre:

> The first time I went into TVC, in 1987 as a young Regional Station Assistant sent up from BBC Southampton to collect some film, I felt I'd finally arrived at the place I'd always wanted to work. Television Centre was ingrained in the imagination of all children of my generation, thanks to the regular use of its corridors, outside areas and rooftops by *Blue Peter*, *Swap Shop* and *Record Breakers*. To not only be inside the hallowed walls of W12 8QT (aka W12 7RJ – I never did understand why it had two postcodes), but to be in a possession of a staff pass,

was wonderful. I'd have happily ended my career there and then and retired with my exciting memories. But, by the time we shut the doors in 2011, East Tower, like me, was showing its age. The place was not intrinsically lovely, and much of it had given up working properly. Its importance was what it stood for, and we packed up as much of that as we could – the creative spirit of BBC Children's, the continuum of generations of programme makers dedicated to the young audience, and many of the people who give it that spirit – and headed up the M6 to a much more fit-for-purpose home.

MediaCity in Salford is our home, and I've no doubt there are kids watching today who get the same buzz watching Barney Harwood arriving by Sea King helicopter in front of MediaCity studios as I felt watching Roy Castle leading 500 tap dancers around Helios's statue at the Centre.

As Joe suggests, in forging new memories for a new generation, the viewers may not notice the difference. But, for me at least, having worked there for nigh on twenty years, it would seem that, with the closure of Television Centre – that world within a world, a beacon of excellence across the globe, and a fertile factory for the imagination of generations of children – the BBC has undoubtedly relinquished one of its great treasures. It is hard to imagine that anything like it will ever exist again.

Looking back at Play School
Paul R. Jackson

2014 is a special year for *Play School* as, 50 years ago at Riverside Studios, it launched, by default, a new BBC TV channel, BBC Two. The new channel controller for BBC Two, Michael Peacock, looked for gaps in the existing television offering. Peacock had two small boys of his own, and was very aware of the lack of nursery school provision in the UK then. As a result, he allocated a new time slot for the very young: 30 minutes a day, Monday through Friday. BBC Radio's *Listen with Mother* producer, Joy Whitby, was appointed and devised a new daily programme whose title was *Play School*. As original programme advisor, Nancy Quayle, explained, this was because, "Play is the child's first school. This is why it was always two words and not one, as many people still consistently and incorrectly write it today". Part of the daily format established in those early years, that continued in various forms over the next two decades, were the toys, the clock introducing the story chair, and the three windows that offered the young viewer a window on the wider world.

On Monday 20th April 1964, BBC Two was due to begin broadcasting. However a massive power failure at Battersea Power Station that evening knocked out Television Centre in West London and postponed programming until 11am the following morning when *Play School* launched the new channel instead. In 1968 the programme moved from Riverside Studios to TV Centre and, for the next twenty years, it was recorded predominantly in studio TC7, providing excellent training opportunities for directors new to the Children's Department, as well as young technical and floor staff.

As a fan of *Play School*, I was finally allowed a set visit during the recording on Wednesday 20th July 1983 and remember the thrill of walking in and seeing the familiar set including the three windows alongside the famous toys and presenters Carol Chell and Ben Bazell.

Former Producer/Director Peter Ridsdale-Scott explained how, when pitching an idea for one of its 'window' films, Nancy Quayle (known as 'Q') told him how young children didn't look up. "To illustrate this point, she asked me how many wild flowers there were from the tube station to TV Centre, and I said I didn't know. Well, Q always came on public transport and she said that from Shepherd's Bush tube to East Tower there were 38 wild flowers. She made the point very simply - that's what a child would see!"

TVC East Tower was a thirteen-storey office block completed in 1964; for many decades it was occupied mostly by the Children's Department.

Kathy Pearce worked as a designer in 1972 and told me: "The only problem I recall having was crossing from the East Tower across the Ring Road at the back of the Centre and hoping a gust of wind didn't blow over a model for the clock base. Sometimes the *Play School* blocks would disappear to other studios to be used for tea trays, but the scenic workers were very helpful because they had children themselves, and perhaps especially as budgets were not huge."

Mishaps did happen of course.

Presenter Chloe Ashcroft recalled how she got her revenge on Hamble for not sitting up straight: "I got a large knitting needle and stuck it up her bottom as far as her head. She went completely rigid and was much better after that!" Presenter Iain Lauchlan remembered an episode featuring 'tubes': "I was playing a game with the toys. We had them rammed into this large cardboard tube and I had to pull them out of one end, a bit at a time so the audience could guess who was coming out next. All went well, until we had the curly hair of Hamble and when I pulled her out of the tube, her head came off!"

Like other areas of the BBC, the programme had to cope with several strikes during the late '70s and early '80s and a few of these hit the headlines. From May to July 1980 the *Play School* clock stopped its familiar 'tick tock' because of a dispute involving three unions, which lasted eight weeks. This happened again from March to April 1982. Presenter Ben Bazell remembered:

> For years, the AFM would switch the switch to make the turntable go round and reveal what the model was to illustrate that day's story. However, one day the electricians' union said *they* should be switching the switch so, for some programmes, the turntable didn't appear at all, until the dispute was resolved. I recall seeing *Would I Lie To You?* in which it was revealed that one disgruntled fan who wrote in was a six year old David Mitchell, now better known for his comedy partnership with Robert Webb.

Julie Stevens recalled working with Australian, Don Spencer, when, due to a strike, no props or studio lights were allowed to be used and they could only use the sink area and toys.

One could always expect the unexpected it seems. Jillie Sutton worked as a PA on the programme from 1979-1985 and recalled: "In the studio Floella Benjamin was doing some knitting, which she dropped and no one knew how to cast on; this burly sceneshifter said, "Give it 'ere" and proceeded to cast on the necessary stitches with great competence, much to our amusement in the gallery."

Director Penny Lloyd Bennett remembered accompanying Big and Little Ted to a charity fundraising exhibition of famous teddy bears. "I dressed them up with satin bows and they had a seat each in my train compartment. I remember that I transported them back to the East Tower at TV Centre without mishap where they rested, still wearing their bows, on top of a filing cabinet, and were promptly stolen!"

Visiting New Zealand presenter, Janine Barry recalled: "My main memory of working at TV Centre (in 1981) was seeing an old man in the basement sweeping the floor with a broom! I was in a hurry to catch my train and asked him the way out. He began by giving me an answer involving lots of lefts and rights and then at the end he said: "And if you find the exit can you come back and tell me as I have been down here for 20 years!" Only afterwards did it dawn on me that the face looked familiar and that it was the legendary Spike Milligan!"

Many famous names were seen in the 'story telling chair' and presenter Ben Bazell told of a visit from Cilla Black: "She started telling the story in a very posh, constrained voice and was delighted when the director asked her to use her well-known Liverpudlian accent." Wendy Duggan, who looked after the pets for 23 years, told me a story involving K'too and the famous cellist Julian Lloyd-Webber, who was recording another programme. When he arrived at TV Centre, he spoke to the receptionist to get his key for his dressing room and the receptionist apologised saying he would have to share with "K'too". He said it wasn't a problem thinking it was a nice Japanese lady, but got a big surprise, on opening the door, to find a cockatoo in there!

Presenter Mike Amatt remembered an interruption to a recording in 1987:

We had a fire drill and, rather than replace the *Play School* toys into their wheeled and lockable cage where they were normally kept, we decided to hold on to them and take them with us as we went to muster in the forecourt. Mustered outside TV Centre were several household names of the day - Michael Fish, Roy Castle and Barry Norman, I recall, plus us *Play School* presenters with the toys Humpty, Jemima, Big Ted, Little Ted and Poppy.

There was an unwritten law that one would never acknowledge, let alone harass a 'star' if one ever came across one in, say, the lifts. So nobody approached any of the household names, out of respect for their privacy, and quite right too. However, **WE** were the centre of attraction, because all the admin and non-studio people recognised the *Play School* toys and wanted to touch them and be introduced to them. All this time we had been working with the stars."

In 1986, Director of Programmes, Michael Grade sent a memo asking for independent quotas from each department and as *Play School* was 11% of Children's output, it suddenly became the target to be outsourced. It was decided to bring the programme to an end and replace it with *Playdays*, which became the first major independent production for BBC Children's, and was made by Felgate Productions run by ex-*Play School* Editor, Cynthia Felgate. Anna Home explained why she took the decision to end the programme:

> When I returned to the BBC (1986), I had to look at the output overall and decide what needed changing or refurbishing. I knew that *Play School* had run its course, but killing it was sensitive both in the department and outside. I knew that there would be a furoré. It probably would have been better if it had happened earlier, but hindsight is a wonderful thing! Putting the preschool programme out to tender was a neat, if slightly cynical way of dealing with the indie quota.
> It was somewhat ironic that Anna Home, a member of the original production team in 1964, and at that time Head of BBC Children's Programmes, had taken the decision to finally close the *Play School* house forever.

On Wednesday 2nd March 1988, the final *Play School* programme was recorded in TC7 with presenters Iain Lauchlan, Liz Watts and Wayne Jackman closing the doors of the house for the last time. The show was, for many generations of preschool viewers and their parents, an iconic preschool programme that is still remembered 26 years after its final transmission in 1988. In April this year, BBC Two broadcast an entertainment special, called *All About Two*, to celebrate BBC Two's 50th anniversary: it opened, of course, with the *Play School* toys and afterwards contributors like Professor Brian Cox, Dara Ó Briain, Richard Osman, Dave Myers and Deborah Meaden, plus many younger programme runners and researchers, all wanted their photo taken with the toys.

In May 2014 at Riverside Studios, the Children's Media Foundation brought together 150 former presenters, musicians, production team members and Children's Department staff, who were joined by current CBeebies stars Justin Fletcher & Chris Jarvis, to celebrate *Play School*'s 50th anniversary and its legacy for preschool programming from *Balamory* and *Tweenies* to *Tikkabilla* to *Show Me Show Me*. It was a wonderful event to celebrate a wonderful, iconic show, the spirit of which continues in BBC preschool programming to this day.

Afterword
Justin Fletcher

Working in children's television has always been a huge privilege for me as it's a medium that can educate and entertain children in this fast-moving world. Back in the 1970s I grew up watching programmes like *Play School*, *Play Away* and *Trumpton* to name but a few. I now look back at these groundbreaking shows with great fondness. Since those days, the world of children's television has grown and grown. The technology of today means that we - and our children - can all have multi-channel TV, mobile phones and computers at our fingertips, competing for our attention.

But children also need to put down the remote or the mouse so they can dress up, cut out snowflakes and build dens. It's just as important today as it was 50 years ago, when *Play School* first started, for us to continue to create high quality children's programming to fuel extraordinary imaginations.

CONTRIBUTORS

from top left

Michael Algar
David Austin
Kay Benbow
Colin Browne
Louise Bucknole
Cynthia Carter
Barbie Clarke
Tony Collingwood
Beth Cox
Torin Douglas, MBE
Stuart Dredge
Justin Fletcher, MBE
Kelvyn Gardner
Joe Godwin
Stuart Harrison

143

Anna Home, OBE
Paul R. Jackson
Brian Jameson
Rob Keeley
Alex Lewis Paul
Sonia Livingstone
Richard Marson
Gary Pope
Julia Posen

Alison Preston
Helen Simmons
Steve Smith
Mark Sorrell
Marie Southgate
Danny Stack
Cheryl Taylor
Colin Ward
Lynn Whitaker

Michael Algar

Michael Algar has worked for 50 years in the film industry. After years of producing TV commercials and sponsored documentaries, he was appointed first Chief Executive of the Irish Film Board in 1982. In that capacity he supervised the financing of selected feature and documentary films by Irish filmmakers. Also, he represented Ireland on committees in the European Union and the Council of Europe, concerning the development and improvement of film industries in Europe.

Since 1989, at the instigation of Jimmy Murakami, he has specialised in producing animation both for cinema and television. Credits with Jimmy include the feature *Christmas Carol* and TV series *The Storykeepers*. Michael also produced the feature *Joseph, King of Dreams*, as well as the series *Teenage Mutant Ninja Turtles*, *Captain Star*, *Budgie the Little Helicopter*, *The Mad Cows*, and many other projects. He is currently producing mobile game apps as well as TV series.

David Austin

David Austin is the Assistant Director and Head of Policy and Public Affairs at the British Board of Film Classification (BBFC). David is the principal advisor on policy and public affairs to the Director and is responsible for coordinating the BBFC's policy work and managing its public affairs outreach. David is also responsible for managing the BBFC's research, communications and education programmes.

David moved to his present role in 2011 having joined the BBFC in 2003 as an Examiner following a career in the Diplomatic Service, where he served in South Asia, Central Africa and former Yugoslavia.

Kay Benbow

Kay was appointed Controller of CBeebies in May 2010 and is responsible for commissioning content for the under-six demographic across all platforms—TV, online, mobile and radio. Kay has over twenty years of experience in children's programming, primarily at the BBC, but also in the independent sector. Under Kay's leadership, CBeebies continues to be the UK's most popular channel for under-sixes. It is the current BAFTA Channel of the Year - the third time in the past four years that CBeebies has won the award. 2013 saw the launch of the CBeebies Playtime App which, with more than 1m downloads in the first two months, was an instant success. Downloads are now at over 2.5m and continue to climb.

CBeebies remains the only preschool channel committed to original British factual and live-action shows for preschoolers, reflecting their real lives and those of their families and communities. Two dramas, featuring children in the lead roles, have brought a new genre to CBeebies: something Kay has worked towards for some years. *Katie Morag* and *Topsy & Tim* achieved excellent ratings (outperforming slot averages) and wide critical acclaim in November 2013.

Kay remains passionate about providing the very best content across all platforms for the BBC's youngest audience by working with in-house production, independent producers and international partners. Kay studied Theology at Oxford University, is married with two sons, and is a proud Arsenal supporter!

Colin Browne

Colin Browne is Chairman of the Voice of the Listener and Viewer, the leading consumer organisation campaigning for quality and diversity in public broadcasting. Previously, he was Director, Corporate Affairs and a member of the Executive Committee at the BBC; Director of Corporate Relations and of Broadband Services at BT plc; and a partner in the Maitland Consultancy, one of London's leading corporate and financial public relations agencies. He now has his own consultancy, providing strategic communications advice. He a is non-executive director of the Centre for Effective Dispute Resolution and a trustee of the Edinburgh Unesco City of Literature Trust. He was previously a member of Ofcom's Communications Consumer Panel.

Louise Bucknole

Louise Bucknole is Director of Programming, Disney Channels UK & Ireland, leading the creation and management of programme and scheduling strategies across the multiplex, on-demand and non-linear platforms, ordering all Disney Channel, Disney Junior and Disney XD content and shaping the overall editorial output.

Louise returned to Disney having previously worked as Senior Manager Programme Planning for Disney Channels UK & Ireland from her former post as Head of Scheduling, BBC Children's, where she oversaw CBBC, CBeebies, the children's blocks on BBC One, BBC Two and iPlayer, and prior to that as Channel Editor and Scheduler for CITV.

Cynthia Carter

Cynthia Carter is senior lecturer in the Cardiff School of Journalism, Media and Cultural Studies, Cardiff University, UK. She has written widely on children, news and citizenship; children's contributions to online discussion boards; citizen journalism and human rights issues in Palestine; news, gender and power; and media violence. She is co-author of *Violence and the Media* (2003) and recently co-edited *Routledge Companion to Media and Gender* (2014) and *Current Perspectives in Feminist Media Studies* (2013). She is founder co-Editor of *Feminist Media Studies* and editorial board member of numerous journals, including the *Journal of Children and Media*. Email: cartercl@cardiff.ac.uk

Barbie Clarke

Dr Barbie Clarke completed her PhD in child and adolescent psychosocial development at the University of Cambridge, Faculty of Education, where her research has looked at early adolescents' use of digital media. A trained child therapist, she has worked with young offenders and in secondary schools. A Fellow of the MRS, Barbie regularly gives papers at international conferences, writes articles, and has appeared on TV and radio commenting on youth research. Barbie heads up social and market research agency Family Kids & Youth (FK&Y) which works on many global research projects with children and young people. FK&Y has been appointed onto the new government roster for market research and is the evaluator for Tablets for Schools and the Youth United Social Action Journey Fund. Barbie is spokesperson for the Market Research Society (MRS) on children's research.

Tony Collingwood

Tony is Writer/Director at Collingwood & Co. He has been making animated children's series through his own company since 1988. His credits include *Harry and His Bucketful of Dinosaurs*, *The Secret Show* and *The Cat in the Hat Knows a Lot About That!* He is currently writing and directing *Ruff-Ruff, Tweet & Dave* - a CGI preschool series - for CBeebies in the UK, and Sprout in the US.

Beth Cox

An inclusion, diversity and equality specialist, Beth Cox has worked in the publishing industry for over a decade. She worked at Child's Play (International) Ltd for more than seven years before leaving to go freelance as an editor and consultant (helping publishers to produce books that are more representative of society as a whole). Beth, along with Alex Strick, is one of the founders of Inclusive Minds – a collaborative project promoting inclusion, diversity, equality and accessibility in children's literature – and, as part of this organisation, she has been involved in various panel and public speaking events, including at the Palace of Westminster; developed and delivered training; and guest-edited a special diversity edition of Write 4 Children Journal. Inclusive Minds recently hosted a ground-breaking day of events at Imagine Children's Festival, which, amongst other things, enabled children to work with illustrators to literally put themselves in the picture.

Natasha Crookes

Natasha is the Director of Communications and Public Affairs for the British Toy and Hobby Association (BTHA). After leaving Liverpool John Moores University with a degree in Sports Science, Natasha worked in events for eight years: firstly, for a fitness company, followed by a Sports Promotions company during a year in Australia. On her return, Natasha worked for a private members club in Pall Mall and joined the BTHA to initially work as the Head of Toy Fair. Natasha has worked for the association for twelve years and in her current position since 2007. Natasha's current role involves identifying opportunities to support the reputable toy companies that make up BTHA membership, and to promote toys and play. Two extremely naughty beagles, a naughty husband and a very well behaved niece and nephew provide the play opportunities in Natasha's life! She can be contacted at Natasha@btha.co.uk
BTHA website – www.btha.co.uk
Make Time 2 Play website – www.maketime2play.co.uk
(also on twitter, Facebook, and a free app)

Torin Douglas, MBE

Torin Douglas has reported on media issues for 40 years, including 24 years as the media correspondent for BBC News until 2013. Before joining the BBC, he worked for the Independent Broadcasting Authority, *The Times*, *The Independent*, and *The Economist* and presented LBC Radio's media show, *Advertising World*. He was awarded the MBE in 2013 for services to the community in Chiswick, where he runs the Chiswick Book Festival and other events – which were actively supported by Richard Briers. He has an Honorary Doctorate from the University of West London and is visiting professor in media at the University of Bedfordshire. He is married with three children and two grandchildren, and is reacquainting himself with children's media.

Stuart Dredge

Stuart is a journalist based in the UK, writing mainly for *The Guardian* (about technology) and *Music Ally* (about the music industry). He also co-founded and edits the Apps Playground website, which reviews new children's apps for iOS and Android. The site published its first e-book – *Apps Playground's 100 Best iPad Apps for Kids* – on Apple's iBooks store early in 2014. He speaks and moderates regularly at conferences, and lives in Henham, Essex, with his family.

Justin Fletcher, MBE

Since graduating from the Guildford School of Acting, Justin has been working as an actor, children's television presenter and voice over artist for the last 21 years. His credits include *Tikkabilla*, *Fun Song Factory*, *Higgledy House* and many more. *Something Special* won the Royal Television Society award for best early years programme for two years running and *CBeebies Springwatch* won a BAFTA for best preschool programme. Currently Justin is presenting *Something Special Out and About* featuring the hugely popular Mr Tumble. He has also just started filming series three of his hugely popular sketch show *Gigglebiz* for CBeebies, playing all twenty six characters himself!

Justin has just finished his arena tour, Justin and Friends, playing to over 100,000 people in two weeks including selling out at Wembley arena. He also has many panto credits and has his own production company, Scrumptious House, which he started fourteen years ago with the aim of creating high quality children's television, video and theatre productions.

In 2008 Justin won a BAFTA for best children's television presenter and was awarded an MBE for his services to children's television and the charity sector. In November 2010, *Something Special* won the BAFTA for best preschool programme and Justin won his second BAFTA for best children's television presenter; in February 2011 *Something Special* won best preschool programme at the *Broadcast* awards. In 2012, *Justin's House* won the BAFTA for best preschool programme and Justin won his third BAFTA for best children's presenter - making him the most awarded children's presenter on Television!

Kelvyn Gardner

Kelvyn has been involved in the international licensing business for over thirty years. After working successfully with an Italian children's publisher, Kelvyn and three colleagues started Merlin Publishing in 1989 to market licensed stickers and trading cards. The company grew throughout Europe and in just five years annual sales reached US $80 million. Merlin was the UK's fastest-growing private company in 1995.

Since 1998, Kelvyn has worked as a consultant in the licensing industry through his company, Asgard Media. At the 2013 Licensing Awards in London, Kelvyn was presented with the Honorary Achievement Award for his work in licensing. Kelvyn has spoken at conferences in London, Manchester, Frankfurt, Milan, Paris, New York, Dubai, Hong Kong, Delhi and Tokyo. He speaks good Italian, competent French and Spanish, and basic conversational Japanese. Since 2006 he has held the mantle of Managing Director of the UK division of LIMA, the Licensing Industry Merchandisers Association. Kelvyn is also a trustee of the Light Fund, the licensing industry's independent charity.

Joe Godwin

As Director of BBC Children's, Joe Godwin heads the world's leading producer and broadcaster of public service children's content. He's responsible for all of the BBC's services for children - CBBC and CBeebies, the UK's most successful children's TV channels, their websites and mobile apps, as well as co-production and commercial partnerships. After reading History at Manchester University, Joe joined the BBC in 1986, working at BBC Southampton in regional news. In 1989 he joined the Children's Programmes department as a Trainee Assistant Producer, studio director and producer on shows such as *Blue Peter*, *Going Live* and *Record Breakers*. From 1997-2000 he was Editor of Children's Presentation. In 2000 he moved to Nickelodeon UK, holding a number of posts including Head of Original Production and VP Interactive Director.

Joe returned to the BBC in 2005 as Head of Children's Entertainment. In 2009 he took up his current post as Director Children's, and in 2011 led the move of the entire Children's Department to its new home at MediaCityUK in Salford. Joe is a member of the BAFTA Children's Committee, The Advisory Panel on Children's Viewing of the British Board of Film Classification, and is a Trustee of the National Museums Liverpool.

Stuart Harrison

Fun Crew create dynamic, original and marketable content for children's media. We're an independent studio, founded in 2006 by writer, Angela Salt, and award-winning character designer, Stuart Harrison. Our passion is for engaging characters, humour and FUN, story-driven ideas which will work universally to entertain across media. We're currently working with a global partner, Technicolor, developing our idea for an adorable, animated comedy series for children aged four to seven, called *Cosmo, Bud & Boo*.

We're interested in building relationships with diverse international co-production partners, broadcasters, publishers and digital media specialists. Fun Crew have an exciting development slate which includes animated shows for preschool to young teen audiences and great ideas for broadcast, games and publishing. We also work with companies as creative consultants to develop new projects.

Anna Home, OBE

Anna is Chair of the CMF Board and a Founding Patron of the organisation. Anna joined BBC radio in 1960 and started in Children's Television in 1964 where she worked as a researcher, then Director, Producer and Executive Producer, latterly specialising in Children's Drama. She started *Grange Hill*, the controversial school series. From 1981-86 she worked at the ITV company TVS where she was Deputy Director of Programmes. In 1986 she returned to the BBC as Head of Children's Programmes, responsible for all children's output. She revived the Sunday teatime classic dramas and one of her last decisions before retiring was to commission *Teletubbies*. After retiring from the BBC, Anna was Chief Executive of The Children's Film & Television Foundation until it merged into CMF in 2012. Anna has won many awards including a BAFTA lifetime achievement award. She was the first chair of the BAFTA Children's Committee, has chaired both the EBU Children's and Youth Working Group and the Prix Jeunesse International Advisory Board. Anna was the Chair of the Save Kids' TV Campaign Executive Committee and the Showcomotion Children's Media Conference, and now chairs the Board of the Children's Media Conference, and is a Board member of Screen South.

Paul R. Jackson

Paul's love of children's television started as a viewer in the late 1960s with favourites including *Play School* and *Camberwick Green*. He worked for the BBC from 1984 and in 1993 was asked to lead the new Duty Office team at ITV's Carlton TV until 2001. Since 1998 he has worked freelance as stage manager on nearly 150 award shows and, in 2014, was on the organising committee for *Play School*'s fiftieth anniversary event.

From 2002-09, Paul worked in hospitality, organising major conferences and weddings at venues, including Leeds Castle and the Holiday Inn, and, from 2010, has worked as a porter at Albany in Piccadilly. Paul is the *Play School* Archivist and author of "Here's A House - A Celebration of *Play School*" Volumes One (1960-79) & Two (From 1980). Available from publishers direct: http://www.kaleidoscopepublishing. co.uk/books-playschool1.html

Brian Jameson

Brian Jameson trained as an actor at RADA. He appeared in his first leading role in Olivier's National Theatre Company at the Old Vic and continued to work in theatres throughout the country. His first TV appearance was in *Warship* for the BBC and then enjoyed many roles in both drama and comedy including *Only Fools and Horses* and *The Les Dawson Show*. He played Brian Epstein in the cult movie *Birth of the Beatles* and later became a presenter on *Play School*. Through his writing Brian started directing for TV and established himself as a leading children's TV Producer. He won a BAFTA, Scottish BAFTA and a Broadcast Award for his creation of the ever-popular *Balamory*. Together with fellow producer Helen Doherty he set up Tattiemoon, a production company in Glasgow. Here they produced *Me Too*, the 150 episode preschool drama series and, more recently, *Woolly & Tig* for CBeebies.

Rob Keeley

Rob Keeley is the author of *The Alien in the Garage and Other Stories*, *The (Fairly) Magic Show and Other Stories* and *The Dinner Club and Other Stories*, all published by Matador, an imprint of Troubador Publishing. His first novel for children, a ghost story called *Childish Spirits*, is now available. Rob has previously written fiction and non-fiction for various periodicals, and has also written for the BBC Radio series for adults, *Chain Gang*, and *Newsjack*. He has recently completed a Master's in Creative Writing from Lancaster University and is increasingly in demand for visits to schools, libraries and literary festivals. For more information on Rob and his books for children, visit www.robkeeley.co.uk For more information about self-publishing, visit the website of *Self Publishing Magazine*: www.selfpublishingmagazine.co.uk

Alex Lewis Paul

Alex is a central government civil servant working in change programme management, who enjoys running occasional half marathons and skiing once a year slightly too fast. She started her working life as an academic researcher in Environmental Geophysics, with a sideline in postgraduate student representation at the Quality Assurance Agency for Higher Education and the European Commission, undertaking committee work on mobility of researchers across Europe's public and private sectors, and the 'brain drain' or 'leaky pipeline' of women at senior lecturer level. She has been a commissioned Army Reserve officer, commanding a troop of twenty, reservist, explosive ordnance disposal soldiers (some in training and some returned from operations in Iraq and Afghanistan). She helped to set up Let Toys Be Toys when she had a son of three and another child on the way, having realised that her own career and interests would be placed almost completely in the 'boys' aisle.

Sonia Livingstone

Sonia Livingstone teaches and researches in the Department of Media and Communications at LSE. She is author or editor of seventeen books and many academic articles and chapters, including *Media Regulation* (2012, with Peter Lunt), *Children, Risk and Safety Online* (2012, edited with Leslie Haddon and Anke Goerzig), and *Meanings of Audiences* (2013, edited with Richard Butsch). Taking a comparative, critical and contextualised approach, Sonia's research asks why and how the changing conditions of mediation are reshaping everyday practices and possibilities for action and identity in public and private spheres. She directs a 33-country network, EU Kids Online, funded by the EC's Safer Internet Programme. She also directs The Class, as part of the MacArthur Foundation-funded Connected Learning Research Network. See http://www.lse.ac.uk/media%40lse/WhosWho/AcademicStaff/SoniaLivingstone/soniaLivingstone.aspx

Richard Marson

After graduating from the University of Durham in 1987, Richard Marson joined the BBC and progressed from floor assistant to producer/director. He spent a decade on *Blue Peter*, where he was Editor for four years and, during this time, won a BAFTA. In 2007, he was Executive Producer of BBC Four's *Children's TV On Trial*. More recently, he produced and directed a 90-minute documentary for BBC Four, *Tales of Television Centre*. He is currently an Executive Producer with TwoFour where he has produced a major fifteen-part 'fixed rig' documentary for CBBC called *Our School* and is now working on a major upcoming 'fixed rig' series for Sky One.

He is the author of several books, including *Inside Updown: The Story of Upstairs, Downstairs*, *Blue Peter 50th Anniversary* and *JN-T: The Life and Scandalous Times of John Nathan-Turner*, and the forthcoming *Drama and Delight: The Life and Legacy of Verity Lambert*.

Gary Pope

Gary is Director, Kids Industries. He trained as an English teacher and led a department before taking a position with a Change Management agency as a facilitator and learning designer working with Eriksson, Thomson, Reuters, BA, Diageo and Disney.

Whilst working for Disney In 1999, Gary realised the opportunity to create Kids Industries . Today KI works from offices in London and CapeTown with Random House, Egmont, Mattel, GSK, Kellogg, CPLG, DHX, eOne Entertainment, Warner Brothers, Al Jazeera and Disney amongst its clients.

Gary is a speaker at conferences worldwide and writes many articles about the modern commercial environment of childhood. He is a Children's BAFTA Juror and the recipient of two IPA Special Awards for Strategy and Effectiveness. Over the last 18months he has led a cross-functional team to redevelop Al Jazeera's seven to twelve Children's Channel into the 360 degree integrated and multi-platform proposition, JeemTV, and the redevelopment of *Peppa Pig*'s global digital presence including the creation of two Number 1 App Store apps.

Gary maintains his interest in education as a school governor.

Julia Posen

Julia Posen has worked at Walker Books for four years. She is responsible for building new business opportunities for the Group Rights and Development division. This is a global team committed to shaping Walker Group properties and products in the development, exploitation, marketing, and sale of auxiliary rights.

Working closely with Helen McAleer on Walker Productions (the in-house production company set up in 2007) Julia has exec produced popular shows such as the animated *Tilly and Friends*, based on the successful books by Polly Dunbar, with JAM Media. The show launched on CBeebies in 2012 and has been sold to over 24 territories globally. Recently Julia has exec- produced the live-action drama *Hank Zipzer* with Kindle Entertainment. Based on Henry Winkler's books, this launched on CBBC in 2014, series 2 is currently in production.

Julia spent twelve years at the BBC, holding a number of senior posts, including Children's Commercial Director at BBC Worldwide.

Alison Preston

Alison Preston is head of media literacy research at Ofcom, the independent regulator and competition authority for the UK communications industries. She leads Ofcom's media literacy research, which provide a wealth of data on the media habits and opinions of children aged three to fifteen and their parents, and adults aged sixteen plus, interviewing over 6,000 people annually. Ofcom's media use and attitudes reports show trends since 2005 in the areas of take-up and use of different media, with a particular focus on internet habits and attitudes. She is a member of the UKCCIS evidence group.

She joined Ofcom in 2003, and previously worked as a research consultant in digital media policy and independent TV production business models. She has a doctorate from the University of Stirling which examined the development of the UK's TV news industry, and has carried out a number of multi-country analyses of TV news coverage of conflicts.

Helen Simmons

Helen is a 39 year old mother of two. Originally from Wigan, she now lives in a small Lincolnshire market town with her husband, whom she met at University, and their children. Helen is a trained Senior Radiographer and works three days a week at the local hospital. Helen's oldest child, six years, attends the nearby primary school and after school club. The care of Helen's youngest child, two and a half years, is split between nursery and grandparents. Helen is a keen baker and often supports her husband's cricket team by providing the teas. A firm fan of socialising with friends, Helen has temporarily hung up her wine glass and is in training for a 10K run to raise money for Cancer Research UK.

Steve Smith

Steve Smith runs Beakus animation studio in London. He is a producer and director, and graduate of the MA Animation course at the Royal College of Art. Over fourteen years of animation creation and production, Steve's work has won a BAFTA (*CBBC Newsround* 'On Poverty'), a British Animation Award (Bibigon 'Fun Facts') and Annecy Crystals. His films include *Eating For Two* (Channel 4, 2002) and *Leap of Faith* (MTV, 2005), whilst his commercial clients include the BBC, Nickelodeon, Google, Kindle, Rankin, RED, McCann Erickson, and The Science Museum.

Steve was the animation director/producer of the CBeebies show *Numtums* (25 x 5-mins). He has helmed the production of an ongoing series of 1-minute seasonal idents for CBeebies, the animated sections of CBBC's *Totally Rubbish* and CBeebies' *Minibeast Adventure with Jess* series. Steve is also collaborating with author/illustrator Leigh Hodgkinson to create an animated preschool show, *Toggle* (52 x 5-mins), which has been pre-bought by CBeebies.
He can often be found lecturing at several universities, judging for BAFTA and the British Animation Awards, and travelling between London and Lewes where he lives. www.beakus.com

Mark Sorrell

Mark Sorrell is a consultant and advisor on freemium game design, behavioural change, value perception and strategy. He has over a decade of experience in making games do new things, in new places, for new audiences, with an enviable history of successful projects for companies across gaming, broadcasting, advertising and finance.

Marie Southgate

As Team Leader of the children's online games project, Marie Southgate was responsible for leading the Office of Fair Trading's investigation and producing the Industry Principles that give guidance to games developers and platforms on their legal obligations. She represents the UK on a European working group of consumer enforcement agencies to ensure that the law relevant to children's online games is interpreted and applied in a consistent and coordinated way across the EU. Marie continues to lead this work in her current role at the Competition and Markets Authority, which she joined when it replaced the OFT on 1 April 2014.

Before joining the OFT, Marie gained experience in other consumer protection roles, including as a Senior Policy and Regulation Manager at the Ministry of Justice, and as a Code Policy Executive at the Advertising Standards Authority's Committee of Advertising Practice. Marie is currently studying law in her spare time.

Danny Stack

Danny Stack has recently written an episode for the new *Thunderbirds Are Go!* for CiTV. His other credits in children's TV include *Fleabag Monkeyface* and *The Amazing Adrenalini Brothers* (CiTV), and *Roy* and *Octonauts* for CBBC. He's also written for *EastEnders* and *Doctors*, and written and directed four short films, one of them an award-winning horror. Since 2005, he's been writing a popular blog called Scriptwriting in the UK www.dannystack.com/blog, which inspired him to set up the Red Planet Prize with TV legend Tony Jordan to help find and encourage new writers. His new original IP is called *Who Killed Nelson Nutmeg?* and if you'd like to know more (or even get involved or support the project), please visit www.nelsonnutmeg.com or email danny@nelsonnutmeg.com

Cheryl Taylor

Despite a sober Quaker upbringing, Cheryl has always loved Drama and Entertainment and embarked on a media career in 1987 as a VT Editor at McCann Erickson London. She worked her way into a commissioning role at Channel 4 via stints in Comic Relief and BBC Entertainment. At Channel Four, Cheryl commissioned *Spaced* and *Black Books*, as well as the first Derren Brown extravaganza in 2000.

After a spell as Head of Comedy at Hat Trick Productions, Cheryl returned to the BBC comedy department and became Controller in 2009 and commissioned *Mrs Brown's Boys*, *The Wrong Mans*, *Citizen Khan*, *Twenty Twelve* and *Bad Education*, amongst others. Cheryl was appointed Controller of CBBC in September 2012 and continues the grand tradition of commissioning inspiring content for children aged six to twelve across the UK. CBBC shows aim to reflect and reveal life experiences and viewer participation plays a key part in its public service offering. Recent commissions include *Our School*, *Hank Zipzer*, *All at Sea*, *Ludus* (CBBC's first play along series), and *The Dog Ate My Homework*.

Colin Ward

Colin Ward is a Writer/Director/Producer with extensive experience of working in children's media production. He started in children's TV with Yorkshire Television, working across factual, entertainment and drama formats. He won a BAFTA for *The Scoop* before joining Granada Kids to produce the BAFTA-nominated game show *Jungle Run*. Moving to the BBC, he won a second BAFTA for the game show *Raven*, going on to work as an Executive Producer with CBBC Scotland on a range of entertainment and drama. More recently, he has combined freelance writing and directing with teaching. He is a member of the Executive Group of the Children's Media Foundation and has responsibility for its links with the research

Lynn Whitaker

Lynn is a lecturer in cultural policy and cultural industries at Centre for Cultural Policy Research, University of Glasgow, and her research straddles all aspects of media production from policy to audience. Her PhD was a production study of BBC Scotland children's department and she is Editor of *The Children's Media Yearbook*. Lynn's most current research is into children's in-app purchasing, and she is interested in developing further knowledge exchange with creative industries. She is a Fellow of the RSA and a trustee of the VLV: in that capacity she finds herself asked to commentate on the future of Scottish broadcasting post-referendum. Lynn is a keen swimmer and enjoys ballroom and Latin dancing.